The Hebrew Bible is hard for modern Latter-day Saints to read and understand. Not only was it written thousands of years ago in a world foreign to the modernity we live in, but we also read it through two thousand years of accumulated Christian understanding and two hundred years of LDS understanding. But even if we can't read it as it was originally written, in *Hope and Healing in the Hebrew Bible: What Ancient Texts Can Teach Modern Readers*, Michael Huston shows us how to capture and understand the power and awe of the Hebrew Bible. After reading this book, I'm excited to reread the Bible. I have new tools for seeing the parts I'm familiar with with new eyes and finding value in the parts I'm less familiar with.

—Sam Brunson
Author of *Between the Temple and the Tax Collector: The Intersection of Mormonism and the State*

A gentle introduction to "Gentile" scholarship on the Old Testament for Latter-day Saints. While writing with members of the Church of Jesus Christ of Latter-day Saints clearly in mind, and frequently referencing sermons and writings by General Authorities, Michael Huston introduces readers to important scholars like Walter Brueggeman, Amy-Jill Levine, Marc Zvi Brettler, Michael Coogan, and Kate Bowler. This beautifully balanced approach succeeds in its aim of showing that reading the Old Testament/Hebrew Bible/Tanakh through multiple interpretive traditions deepens and enriches the ways that Latter-day Saint Christians can understand these writings. He reads some familiar sections—creation, exodus, David and Bathsheba—and some that we tend to skip over—Leviticus, the story of Huldah, the Psalms—in ways that both honor and challenge conventional LDS readings. This book will reinvigorate your Sunday School preparation or perhaps even teach you how to love the Old Testament for the first time!

—Kristine Haglund
Author of *Eugene England: A Mormon Liberal*

The Hebrew Bible is the lengthiest, most daunting, least studied, and least understood of all books in the Latter-day Saint canon. *Hope and Healing in the Hebrew Bible* demystifies this great scripture and invites us to consider it normatively, rather than defensively. That is, rather than use is to justify and defend Latter-day Saint doctrines formulated several millennia later, the author suggests that we accept it on its own terms and in its own context of time and place, without the clutter of LDS apologetics. Only when we cease to "Mormonize" the Hebrew Bible do we gain entrée into its most profound content.

—Gregory A. Prince
Author of *David O. McKay and the
Rise of Modern Mormonism* and
*Leonard Arrington and the Writing
of Mormon History*

HOPE & HEALING
IN THE HEBREW BIBLE

BCC
PRESS

BY COMMON CONSENT PRESS is a non-profit publisher dedicated to producing affordable, high-quality books that help define and shape the Latter-day Saint experience. BCC Press publishes books that address all aspects of Mormon life. Our mission includes finding manuscripts that will contribute to the lives of thoughtful Latter-day Saints, mentoring authors and nurturing projects to completion, and distributing important books to the Mormon audience at the lowest possible cost.

HOPE & HEALING

IN THE HEBREW BIBLE

*What ancient texts can teach
modern readers.*

MICHAEL HUSTON

For information contact
By Common Consent Press
972 East Burnham Lane
Draper, Utah 84020

Cover design: D Christian Harrison
Cover art: "The Teachings," Abby Huston, 8″ × 11″, Paper collage on
    Bristol board
Book design: Andrew Heiss

www.bccpress.org

ISBN-13: 978-1-961471-30-6

10 9 8 7 6 5 4 3 2 1

This book is dedicated to my wife and children who have supported me, given me encouragement, and patiently tolerated my habit of working through ideas out loud.

I want to express my deepest appreciation to Eric Lacey for (again!) providing me invaluable insight and support in his careful review of early drafts of this book. And a special note of appreciation to Michael Austin and all the wonderful people who make BCC Press possible. I am so grateful you were willing to help make this book a reality.

Contents

CONTENTS

Introduction[1]

I always used to feel a little bit anxious when Sunday School cycled back around to the Old Testament. My anxiety came from two places: First, the sheer enormity of the Old Testament—it is more than twice as long as the New Testament. How was I ever going to read through the whole thing? And second, the seeming impenetrability of some of the language—it was a maze of unfamiliar people, geography, and teachings. People joke about the Isaiah chapters in 2 Nephi being hard to read. For me, the writings of Isaiah felt at least somewhat approachable when compared to parts of Deuteronomy and Leviticus.

So, at the beginning of each four-year Old Testament cycle, I committed to read the verses identified in the Sunday School student material and hoped that I would come away with something that made the effort worthwhile. That worked for me, until it didn't. At some point, and I don't quite remember when, it dawned on me that the Old Testament must be more than a collection of seemingly haphazardly scattered verses pulled from the middle of very long sections of text which served (primarily) to support Latter-day Saint (LDS) doctrines and practices. These ancient teachings had sustained the an-

---

1. Portions of this chapter, now modified, appeared in *Public Square Magazine* on January 11, 2022: https://publicsquaremag.org/faith/gospel-fare/Latter-day-saints-need-the-old-testament/

cient Israelites and modern-day Jews through invasions, deportations, persecutions, and the horrors of the Holocaust. Yet, as I read through these scriptures, I found myself struggling to understand what was happening, and I sometimes found myself fighting just to stay awake in Sunday school. "I must be missing something," I thought. This realization about the Old Testament came at a time in my life when I was, more generally, reconsidering my overall approach to belief and faith.

Largely as a result of encouragement from my wife, I finally acted on a prompting that I had been feeling for a long time and began to pursue a master's degree at Wesley Theological Seminary, a Methodist seminary in Washington, DC. The very first class for which I registered was "Introduction to the Old Testament." Taught in two sections by two different professors (both well-known and respected in the world of Old Testament scholarship), these survey courses helped the Old Testament come alive to me. I realize now, it came alive because I finally stopped trying to find the ways in which the Old Testament reinforced my existing perspectives and started allowing the Old Testament to teach me. That is to say, I started to accept the Old Testament for exactly what it was and sought to read and understand it on its own terms. And what it offered was as unexpected as it was profound. It was, in fact, life giving. It is impossible to emphasize strongly enough the impact that the Old Testament had, and continues to have, in my life. I entered Wesley at a time of great spiritual tumult in my own life, and it is no overstatement to say that the Old Testament saved my faith.

Now, I am not suggesting that attending a seminary is right for everyone. And I am not suggesting that my experience with the Old Testament is normative. The fact that I had the time and resources to attend a top-notch theological seminary is a privilege for which I will always be grateful. And the fact that the Old Testament had such a profound impact on me likely says more about me than it does about the Old Testament.

What I *am* suggesting is that during my time at Wesley one of the things I learned is that we, the LDS community and Christians more generally, need the Old Testament more than we may realize. And if that book of scripture is to be transformative, then our familiarity with it needs to extend beyond the ability to find the few verses that we think support what we already believe—we need the whole Megillah. What's more, we need to allow ourselves to be surprised by what it says and to allow ourselves to find nourishment in unexpected places (being surprised and finding nourishment in unexpected places are both common themes in the Old Testament!). Such an approach is, I believe, central to our faith collectively and a critical foundation for personal growth. And, in ways that are non-trivial, LDS beliefs may be more reliant on Old Testament foundations than many other Christian denominations. For instance:

⁍ **PROPHETS** The LDS notion of a prophet is grounded in the Old Testament. The Old Testament not only provides a variety of different examples for how prophetic leadership looks, it also shows a variety in the prophetic voice and the many surprising ways God works through those called to speak God's word. Of all Christian denominations, the LDS faithful need a more thoughtful grounding in prophetic literature because we sustain modern-day prophets, seers, and revelators as a formal part of our ecclesiastical structure.

⁍ **ABRAHAM AND THE HOUSE OF ISRAEL** As President Russell M. Nelson articulated in multiple ways in the years preceding his passing, the Abrahamic Covenant looms large in everything we do in the LDS Church. That covenant is both articulated for the first time in, and embodied throughout, the Old Testament. It is in the Old Testament that we see how this covenant plays out for Abraham and then for his descendants.

Further, it is only in the Old Testament that the specific promises given to each of the sons of Jacob/Israel are recorded (Genesis 49, cf. Deuteronomy 33)—something tied closely to the LDS practice of receiving patriarchal blessings. Though the Pearl of Great Price does offer some insight on these topics, the fact remains that most of what we know about the Abrahamic Covenant specifically and the House of Israel generally comes from the Old Testament.

⁘ **FOUNDATIONAL SACRED TEXT** First, scriptures unique to the LDS church are rooted in the Old Testament. For the Book of Mormon, a familiarity with Old Testament teachings and stories is assumed. There is no explanation of the Abrahamic Covenant in the Book of Mormon; it simply assumes that the reader already knows what that is. The Pearl of Great Price's Book of Moses owes its existence to Joseph Smith's reading of the Old Testament. Even the Doctrine and Covenants, a decidedly modern text, contains numerous revelations in which God both self-identifies and also describes the early LDS faithful with language pulled directly from the Old Testament (see for example: 8:3, 36:1; 50:44; 61:25; 103:16–17; 109:1; 136:21). If this reliance on the Old Testament is not enough, second, Jesus expressly taught from the texts that now make up the Old Testament. For example, Jesus's teaching about the two greatest commandments, to love God and love our neighbor, comes directly from Deuteronomy 6:4–5 and Leviticus 19:18, respectively. In Matthew's account of Jesus refuting the devil's temptations after his forty-day fast (Matt 4:1–11), Jesus does so with Old Testament teachings (mostly from Deuteronomy). When Jesus cleanses the temple, He cites language found in Isaiah and Jeremiah (Mark

11:15–18; cf. Isaiah 56:7, Jeremiah 7:11). On the cross, Jesus quotes from Psalms (Matt. 27:46; Mark 15:34; Luke 23:46; John 19:28; Psalms 22:1; Psalms 31:5; Psalms 69:21). In short, the story of Jesus makes exceptionally clear that, among other things, Jesus knew and taught from Israel's scriptures. Given the pivotal role that the Old Testament plays in the LDS canon, and Jesus' example of reliance upon Old Testament texts, we need to take every opportunity to learn this book of scripture better.

⊰⊱ **MESSIAHSHIP** Though Christians have understood the notion of "messiah" in ways that are slightly different than their Jewish friends—specifically Christians' seeing Jesus of Nazareth as *The* Messiah"—the idea of *a messiah* (an 'anointed one,' translated as *"chrīstós"* in Greek) comes from, and is most explored in, the Old Testament. The first followers of Jesus, all of whom were Jewish, pulled from this ancient and pre-existing messiah tradition as a way to explain Jesus and to understand Jesus's mission. Our modern views about, and professions of, "Jesus as the Messiah" owe their existence to a reinterpreted Old Testament idea. As is evidenced by Easter classics like Handel's "Messiah" or the Christmas hymn "O Come, O Come Immanuel," Christianity owes much of its liturgical language about Jesus Christ to the Old Testament. As people who see ourselves as carrying modern-day message of The Messiah for the world,[2] better understanding the messianic tradition can only help us.

---

2. "The Living Christ: The Testimony of the Apostles, The Church of Jesus Christ of Latter-day Saints." Available at https://www.churchofjesuschrist. org/study/scriptures/the-living-christ-the-testimony-of-the-apostles/the-living-christ-the-testimony-of-the-apostles.

Obviously, this short list of why the LDS community needs the Old Testament is incomplete, but I hope it is illustrative. And I am optimistic this list drives home the reality that the LDS community, individually and collectively, needs to do much more than proof-text Old Testament verses to support what we already believe. Quite the opposite in fact. Maybe more than all other Christian denominations, LDS beliefs and scripture seem to suggest that the LDS faithful have a *special* obligation to take the time to understand this sacred book, and to understand it on its own terms. We need to dig into the Old Testament with a seriousness and willingness that demonstrates our commitment to the God of Abraham, Isaac, and Jacob and an openness to have our old ideas challenged in order to have new ideas take root. For some of us, this may feel like a first step into the wilderness; but, as we learn in the Old Testament, the wilderness is a place of unexpected manna, water, and meat. The wilderness is the place where we really come to know the God who leads us as under a cloud by day and a pillar of fire by night.

SECTION I

Laying the Groundwork

My approach to the Old Testament affects the way I read and draw meaning from it. So before proceeding into the Old Testament itself I want to be transparent about some aspects of the critical and theological scaffolding that I use. To that end, in this section I will first spend a little time discussing how I approach the text of the Old Testament. And then I will level-set the conversation with some basic background and information about the Old Testament itself. This section is not intended as an introduction to the Old Testament, but I hope that laying this basic groundwork will start the process of demystifying the text (one overarching goal of this project), set the stage for the chapters that follow, and provide a jumping off point for folks who want to delve further into to the Old Testament beyond what is discussed in this book.

CHAPTER 1

What's in a Name?

Old Testament is a contested term. And yet it is the term that is most commonly recognized among the LDS community, and probably among most of Christendom when referring to the book of scripture that Christians inherited from ancient Israel. It is the term I have used so far precisely because of its ubiquity. But I do not think it is a very useful term. So going forward I will stop using the term *Old Testament* and instead call this group of texts the *Hebrew Bible*.[1] And I want to spend a little time exploring why this matters.

When the "Old Testament" is set next to the "New Testament" (as happens in the LDS-sanctioned edition of the Bible), the word "old" takes on connotations that go beyond chronological descriptions, and plants a theological flag in the ground. The old vs new framework effectively asserts (as we see in its nascent form in Hebrews 8:13) that Jesus's coming, teachings, and death recentered the locus of God's engagement with humankind. God's Torah-centered engagement

---

1. *Hebrew Bible* as a term is also problematic for different reasons, not the least of which is that portions of it were originally written in Aramaic (and some Christians denominations also include in their sacred texts apocryphal books that were originally authored in Greek). For a pithy and powerful discussion on this issue see, Amy-Jill Levine and Marc Zvi Brettler, *The Bible With and Without Jesus, How Jews and Christians Read the Same Stories Differently*, pp.7–14.

with the Children of Israel was the old way, and now God's engagement with humankind through Jesus and Christianity is the new way. If we are being honest, this view, in one way or another, is pretty widely held in the LDS community and in Christianity more generally. And it is not surprising that many Latter-day Saints espouse this view; after all, it is a narrative that supports the sense of exceptionalism that permeates much of LDS culture and, more broadly, that reinforces Christianity's sense of privilege when it comes to a relationship with, knowledge about, and access to God. When taken to the extreme, this perspective is called supersessionism.

Supersessionism, in its most pernicious form, holds that Christians replaced (i.e. "superseded") the Children of Israel as God's chosen people.[2] Supersessionism was and is often a central and foundational justification for historical and modern antisemitic rhetoric and actions perpetrated by Christians against the Jewish community. The LDS community is not immune to this idea—in fact, some General Authorities, including J. Ruben Clark, who served as the First Counselor in the First Presidency, perpetuated this damaging narrative.[3] Though I have personally rarely heard such sentiments expressed out loud at local worship services, I have heard them seep into discussions of the "lesser law" (by which the LDS community means the Law of Moses) and the "higher law" (by which the LDS community means the modern-day Restoration form of the Gospel of Jesus). The way this is sometimes voiced in a modern LDS context is something like this: *the Children of Israel were so unfaithful that God took away the higher law and gave them a lesser law, and with Jesus's coming and the Restoration we (the Latter-day Saints) now have (again) the higher*

---

2. Some of the language that follows appeared originally in a post on *By Common Consent*: https://bycommonconsent.com/2023/04/25/avoiding-antisemitism-in-our-discussion-of-the-new-testament/
3. See D. Michael Quinn, *Elder Statesman: A Biography of J. Reuben Clark*, pp. 325–327.

law which is the only path to exaltation, and thus we are now the chosen people taking this new message to the world.[4] In my view, not only is this perspective theologically misguided, but it also requires that one ignore significant scriptural evidence to the contrary—both points which I will address in various ways in the chapters that follow.

I realize that there is some language in the LDS standard works and from General Conference talks that may lead some to take a soft-supersessionist position. Yet, it is also true that such language stands alongside scriptures and General Conference talks that also confirm the indisputable reality that during his Earthly ministry Jesus regularly taught out of the texts that would eventually form the Hebrew Bible. In fact, many of Jesus's most radical, transformational teachings can be firmly grounded in identifiable scriptural passages from ancient Israel (e.g., Matthew 22:37–40 cf. Deuteronomy 6:5, Leviticus 19:17–18). Further, as noted in the introduction, Jesus used Israel's scriptures as the basis for repudiating Satan in the wilderness (Matthew 4:1–11). And additionally, the New Testament Gospel writers regularly lean on the authority of these ancient texts as a basis to establish the veracity of their writings and to support the reality of Jesus's divine mission—i.e. they used the Hebrew Bible as a justification for,

---

4. In many ways, this framing is adapted from Reformed covenant theology which understands a Jesus-centric "covenant of grace" (i.e. the Gospel) to have replaced the ancient "covenant of works" (i.e. the old law). However, Latter-day Saint scripture tends to push against this theological approach. Instead, the Book of Mormon and Doctrine and Covenants both see the covenant with Israel as continually relevant and expanding in modern times (1) to encompass non-Israelites and/or (2) to identify new connections to the covenant through Patriarchal Blessings. Though this carries its own challenges—not the least of which is concern about cultural appropriation—it does mean the LDS theological approach to covenant could be viewed as more consistent with the Hebrew Bible's approach than is Reformed covenant theology.

and explanation of, Jesus's Messianic actions, and to give their own Gospels an authoritative status.

Alongside those realities, the Book of Mormon's description of Jesus's ministry in the Americas includes a record of Jesus's near-verbatim recitation of many prophetic teachings now found in the King James Version of the Hebrew Bible. This language, which was not on the Plates of Brass, was apparently so valuable that Jesus preempted the time he might have spent communicating his own unique teachings to quote and comment upon certain parts of Israel's scriptures. And finally scholars—for instance Amy-Jill Levine and Marc Zvi Brettler—have shown how, time and time again, Jesus's sermons in the New Testament reinforce earlier prophetic teachings (rather than dismissing or overriding them).[5]

Yes, Jesus—whom Christians accept as the Son of God and Savior of the World—was an observant Jew. And though Jesus, at times, took issue with the ways in which some of his contemporaries observed their religious obligations, Jesus was never critical of the scriptural base upon which his faith tradition was built, and Jesus never said or did anything that suggested his followers were to replace (or "supersede") the relationship between God and Israel.[6]

A history of the development of the Christian and Jewish canons is both beyond the scope of this book and unnecessary to make my point (it is, however, fascinating and worthy of additional study for those who are interested). Suffice it to say

---

5. For example, see their analysis of the Sermon on the Mount, and specifically the "antitheses" found in Matthew 5:28–41. They show that in the Sermon on the Mount Jesus was using a known contemporaneous Jewish device for "extending" teachings, not contradicting them or replacing them. See *The Bible With and Without Jesus, How Jews and Christians Read the Same Stories Differently*, 2020 (Harper One: NY, NY): pp. 179–212.
6. This claim is made in later New Testament texts, most prominently in the Epistle to the Hebrews. However, this text was likely composed many years after Jesus's death and thus likely reflects the views of first century Christians more than it does the teachings of Jesus himself.

that early Christians, in an attempt to distinguish the mission and message of Jesus (and the new scriptures that surrounded the origins, development, and maturation of Christianity) from Israel's religious traditions (and the scriptures that undergirded them), called the books of scripture that contained Christian teaching the "New Testament" and called the books of scripture that contained teachings that preceded Jesus the "Old Testament."[7] To wit: *the term Old Testament is a Christian creation.* I have no desire to assign malicious motives to early Christians who created the term, nor to modern Christians who subsequently used it. But malicious or not, the effect is the same: the term functionally serves (1) to elevate Christianity over Judaism, (2) to reframe Israel's scriptures within the context of Christianity, and (3) to appropriate Israel's scriptures by asserting an interpretive framework that effectively invalidates non-Christian readings.

Thus, in our modern time, with the backdrop of centuries of anti-Jewish tendencies[8] that have found their way into Christianity in subtle and not-so-subtle ways, the term "Old Testament" creates a hierarchy of scripture, relegating the Hebrew Bible to second-class status in many Christian houses of worship. After all, why study something old, when you can study something new? Why read the old message when you have the new message? In my view, this approach to the "Old Testament" is like wallpaper that has been up as long as we can remember, and we have become so accustomed to it that

---

7. The first written use of the term "Old Testament" is attributed to Melito of Sardis sometime in the late second century. Its use is attested in the work of the Christian historian Eusebius, *Ecclesiastical History*, 4.26.12, 14; available at: http://www.ccel.org/ccel/schaff/npnf201.iii.ix.xxvi.html

8. Amy-Jill Levine helpfully distinguishes between antisemitic and anti-Jewish; the prior centers on race or ethnicity, whereas the latter centers on theology. See her discussion of this in *The Misunderstood Jew, The Church and the Scandal of the Jewish Jesus.* pp. 87–117.

we do not notice it anymore. Well, it is time to notice this wall-paper and tear it down.

As I note above, I will return to this issue in different ways in some of the chapters that follow and will, I hope, show how this view is fundamentally flawed. But for the purpose of laying the groundwork here, I want to foreground that this is why I will be referring to Israel's scriptures as the Hebrew Bible. In my view "Old Testament" as a term carries too much baggage to be useful and sets up modern readers to misunder-stand the texts from the beginning. By calling it the Hebrew Bible I hope to level (or reset) the playing field a little—since it is a term that helps deemphasize some of the assumptions the LDS community might otherwise bring to the text. From an analytical perspective this means that I will not read and understand the Hebrew Bible as primarily a foreshadowing of Christianity, nor will I view the Hebrew Bible as only (or tru-ly) understandable in the light of Christianity, nor will I treat its teachings as a lesser, incomplete law that is made more complete by Jesus's advent. In sum, I am completely reject-ing the Old-Testament-versus-New-Testament framework. To be clear, I cannot escape my Christian background and make no attempt to try—in fact, as will be clear in the chapters that follow, my LDS Christian background is always present as I ap-proach different aspects of the Hebrew Bible. But throughout this book I will be treating (or, at least, making every effort to treat) the Hebrew Bible as scripture that deserves respect for what it is and as it is, without imposing upon it an anachro-nistic Christian gloss.

CHAPTER 2

Not an Apology

In addition to its common definition as an "admission of error or discourtesy accompanied by an expression of regret," the word apology also means "something that is said or written to defend something that other people criticize."[1] Thus, someone who is actively defending (in word or writing or otherwise) some thing or idea that is being challenged can be said to be an apologist for that thing or idea. As a specific example, people who are defending (in word or writing or otherwise) the LDS Church are apologists for the LDS Church. There is nothing inherently wrong with being an apologist or with creating an apology for some thing or idea that one feels strongly about.[2] Much of the material we encounter as we participate in our LDS faith communities—e.g., the materials in *Come, Follow Me*, General Conference talks, or pro-LDS social media—are, at their core, apologetic in nature: this material is intentionally crafted for the purpose of defending a particular teaching, or approach, or worldview, or standard, etc. It

---

1. "Apology." *Merriam-Webster.com Dictionary*, Merriam-Webster, https://www.merriam-webster.com/dictionary/apology. Accessed 11 Nov. 2024.
2. However, apologetics can become problematic if, in the pursuit of defending a dogma or ideology, one increasingly leans unproven or unsupported ideas, employs logical fallacies, or otherwise ignores information and data that directly contradicts the position being taken.

is wholly unsurprising that information prepared by the LDS Church, or by people who understand themselves speaking as representatives of these beliefs (both formally, like General leadership, or as self-appointed speakers, like on social media), is apologetic. And, to be clear, apology plays a role in the community of believers by providing resources for the community and by standing in defense of that community and what it holds as true.

That said, if it was not already clear—and I want to be very transparent about this—this book is not a Christian or LDS apologetic reading of the Hebrew Bible. As a matter of faith tradition, I come from an LDS background. I served an LDS mission. I have held numerous callings and assignments in the LDS Church. I attend an LDS congregation. That I come to the Hebrew Bible with an LDS Christian background is an inescapable reality, and the traditional understandings that I inherited from that community (both LDS-specific traditions and more general Christian traditions) inform my reading of Hebrew Bible texts, both in ways of which I am aware and in ways of which I am not. However, my goal in this book is not to use the Hebrew Bible to defend Christianity. Neither is my goal to use the Hebrew Bible to attack Christianity. My goal in this book is not to use the Hebrew Bible to defend the LDS Church. Neither is my goal to use the Hebrew Bible to attack the LDS Church. My goal is simply to take the Hebrew Bible seriously and see where that leads me.

Analytically, this means I will sometimes use LDS sources to support a given understanding of the Hebrew Bible and, when it seems justified by the text of the Hebrew Bible itself, I will sometimes ignore common LDS interpretations of specific scriptures. As a result, my analytic observations and conclusions of certain Hebrew Bible texts may or may not align with current LDS understandings of those texts. Given what I have already laid out, perhaps that is unsurprising. However, I often foreground how the LDS community might read or understand certain texts. I do this primarily because (1) I am LDS and these readings and understandings were often my first way of seeing certain texts, and also (2) because those readings and understandings will likely be shared by this book's primary audience. In any instance, I do not claim that my observations and conclusions are fully authoritative to the exclusion of all others; rather, anything that follows should be seen as sitting alongside—and not seen as intentionally supporting, reinforcing, replacing, or contradicting—other readings.

To that point, taking a step back, one overarching goal for this book is to provide some interpretive tools and options for people who may desire to deepen their understanding of the Hebrew Bible but who are unsure where to start. I want this book to be something from which people can build. I hope to do this by providing some basic scaffolding for understanding the Hebrew Bible, and then by modeling some ways of approaching and analyzing specific Hebrew Bible stories and teachings, some of which regularly come up in LDS discussions. My hope is that the chapters that follow will feel fresh. I also hope that they will be deeply grounded in an obvious and evident respect for and love of the Hebrew Bible. I hope to demonstrate the power the Hebrew Bible can bring into the lives of the LDS community when we choose to move beyond pre-prepared lesson material and surface-level discussions that seem more concerned with LDS apologetics than anything else, and instead embrace the Hebrew Bible on its own terms.

In a perfect world, I hope that at the end of this book, readers will feel motivated to leave this book behind so they can begin interacting with, and earnestly striving with, the Hebrew Bible in their own ways.

CHAPTER 3

Different Bibles, Different Stories

Christians are often surprised to learn that the Jewish and Christian versions of the Hebrew Bible are organized differently—that is to say that the books which comprise them are in a different order. These differences in organization are more than just clerical choices. Ordering its various parts differently impacts the way one reads the Hebrew Bible as a whole and, in important ways, changes the overall message of the book of scripture.

The King James Version (KJV) of the Bible carries the institutional support of the LDS Church for English speaking saints. So, the LDS tradition, by using the KJV, accepts the same ordering books as churches in the Protestant tradition (King James was, after all, a Protestant). The modern KJV excludes apocryphal, intertestamental texts which continue to be included in the Catholic and Eastern Orthodox canon.[1] In

---

1. For nearly 275 years, the KJV included apocryphal texts. Those texts were finally removed in the late 19th century (which means that Joseph Smith's Bible included the apocrypha). Separately: for simplicity's sake, and because English is my primary language, I will be framing the conversation within the context of the KJV. However, the non-English versions of the Hebrew Bible that have the institutional support of the LDS church are generally organized the same way as the KJV.

the KJV, the Books of the Hebrew Bible are organized as follows:

-ᛞ- **THE PENTATEUCH**   Genesis, Exodus, Leviticus, Numbers and Deuteronomy. As a matter of tradition, these books are said to have been authored by Moses, but the weight of biblical scholarship suggests otherwise. Rather these texts were likely compiled over a long period of time, reflecting both very old and comparatively recent understandings, interpretation, and traditions which often sit in close proximity to each other. As one example, there are two creation narratives that sit side-by-side: Genesis 1:1–2:4a and Genesis 2:4b–3:24.[2] These different accounts of creation have different points of emphasis, different concerns, use different names for God, and may well reflect traditions informed by different parts of Israel's past (chronologically, geographically, and historically). As a body of texts, the Pentateuch contains various etiologies, or origin stories, for humankind generally and for Israel specifically—so, for instance, these books tell the stories of Noah and Abraham and their families. Additionally, the Pentateuch contains the narrative of Israel's deliverance from Egypt, its experience in the wilderness and at Sinai, and the instructions given by God to Moses to guide Israel's life in the promised land.

---

2. Scholar Jeffrey Geoghegan also observes that there are "two descriptions of Abraham's covenant with God (Gen 15 and Gen 17), two accounts of Jacob's name change to 'Israel' (Gen 32 and Gen 35), and and two versions of Moses's commission to lead the Israelites out of slavery (Exod 3 and Exod 6)." Further, Geoghegan comments on the two different narratives of the flood that also sit in close proximity to each other. See "Two Flood Narratives," *Bible Odyssey*, available at: https://www.bibleodyssey. org/articles/two-flood-narratives/

‡ **THE HISTORIES** Joshua, Judges, Ruth, 1 & 2 Samuel, 1 & 2 Kings, 1 & 2 Chronicles, Ezra, Nehemiah, and Esther. Broadly, these books aim to tell the entire post-Moses history of Israel. From its arrival in and settlement of the promised land, to the establishment and fracturing of the monarchy, to the invasions of the Assyrians and the Babylonians, to the Exile and the rise of Persian power, to the return of Israel back to the land of promise and the reestablishment of Jerusalem. Notably, the history of the monarchy as told in 1 & 2 Samuel and 1 & 2 Kings differs in some ways from 1 & 2 Chronicles, even though it covers the same timeline (for example, the story of David and Bathsheba is excluded from Chronicles). Further, Biblical scholarship suggests that books like Ruth (which supposedly takes place in the time of the Judges) and Esther (which supposedly takes place during the Persian rule), were not contemporaneously written but rather are moralistic stories written at a much later time, but which were set in a specific historical milieu for narrative purposes.

‡ **THE POETRY/WISDOM LITERATURE** Job, Psalms, Proverbs, Ecclesiastes, Song of Solomon. These books aim to capture a variety of distinct kinds of wisdom literature from different times and places. For instance: Psalms is a collection of prayers and songs, some of which may have been very old and some of which may have been used in official settings such as at the enthronement of the king or during certain kinds of worship ceremonies; whereas, Proverbs is a collection of maxims that may have originated, in some form or another, as family or clan "folk sayings" but which were later collected and carefully compiled to form the relatively structured anthology of sayings we cur-

rently have; sayings which range from common sense suggestions for day-to-day life to ruminations on deep mysteries.[3] The LDS community generally does not know what to do with the Song of Solomon; Bruce R. McConkie infamously called it "biblical trash" and compared it to verbal pornography.[4]

⊹⊹ **THE MAJOR PROPHETS** Isaiah, Jeremiah, Lamentations, Ezekiel, Daniel. These books aim to capture the major prophetic influences associated with the time of the Assyrian invasion of the Northern Kingdom (Isaiah, during the 8th century BCE), the Babylonian invasion of the Southern Kingdom, the destruction of Jerusalem and the Temple, and the deportation of many of its inhabitants (Jeremiah, Lamentations, during the late 7th and early 6th centuries BCE), life in exile under Babylonian rule (Ezekiel, during the 6th century BCE), and life in exile within Babylonian, Median, and Persian royal courts (Daniel, also during the 6th century BCE). So, on their face, these books overlap with some of the historical periods which are also captured in 1 & 2 Samuel, 1 & 2 Kings, 1 & 2 Chronicles, Ezra, and Nehemiah. It is worth observing that this historical correlation is not nearly as clean cut as we might like. For instance, portions of Isaiah were likely written during exile, and portions of Daniel (the only Hebrew Bible text that contains language originally composed in Aramaic) may have been written as late as the 2nd century BCE, making Daniel the youngest book of the Hebrew Bible (well after the time of Persian rule, when the narrative in Daniel is set).

---

3. See Bruce C. Birch et al, *A Theological Introduction to the Old Testament, 2nd Ed,* pp.385–400.
4. Dana M. Pike and Eliason, Eric A. "Is the Song of Solomon Scripture?" *BYU Studies Quarterly,* p. 183.

✤ **THE MINOR PROPHETS** Hosea, Joel, Amos, Obadiah, Jonah, Micah, Nahum, Habakkuk, Zephaniah, Haggai, Zechariah, and Malachi. The difference between the major and the minor prophets is primarily length. And, again, there is chronological overlap with the histories and the major prophets. For instance, the books of Isaiah, Micah, Amos, and Hosea, 2 Kings, and 2 Chronicles all contain writings from the 8th century BCE, sometimes presenting different perspectives of the same events. There is similar overlap with writings from the 6th century BCE in the books of Ezekiel, Habakkuk, Obadiah, 2 Kings and 2 Chronicles. To be sure, triangulating the different ways that the same timelines are captured in the histories, the major prophets, and the minor prophets is no mean feat! Organizationally, there was an attempt to place the minor prophets chronologically. There appears to have been an intentional decision on the part of Christians who compiled Hebrew Bible texts to ensure Malachi was the last book. This is likely because Christians understood the reference in Malachi 4:5 to Elijah's return preceding the coming of God to be a prophecy of John the Baptist preceding the advent of Jesus. Thus, Malachi, placed as the last book of the KJV, allowed Christian editors to create a bridge of sorts between the Hebrew Bible and the Gospels.

So, what is the story of the KJV? What is the overarching narrative? From a bird's eye view, the KJV tells the story of God creating the earth, establishing a relationship with a specific group of people, and the exile and return of those people. It concludes with a series of prophetic voices, many of which are interpreted as pointing forward to the coming of Jesus. That is to say, the KJV organizes the Hebrew Bible in such a way that it tells a story that anticipates Jesus's arrival. And many of us who were raised with a Christian background have been taught to understand the Hebrew Bible through this lens. It is unsurprising, I think, that many of us—and specifically many in the LDS community—struggle to read the Hebrew Bible as anything other than a prequel to the New Testament.

But the Jewish version of the Hebrew Bible is organized differently and, thus, tells a different story. The Jewish scriptures are organized into three large sections: The *Torah*, the *Nevi'im*, and the *Kethuvim*. Taken together, this book of scriptures is sometimes called the *Tanakh* (an acronym created by taking sounds from all three sections of the scriptures and combining them).

* **THE TORAH** Genesis, Exodus, Leviticus, Numbers and Deuteronomy. Often clumsily translated into English as "The Law," it is probably better translated as "The Teachings" or "The Instructions." The Torah and the Pentateuch contain the same books. Judaism also traditionally attributes authorship to Moses, but (as is noted above) Biblical scholarship suggests otherwise.

* **THE NEVI'IM** The Nevi'im, "The Prophets"[5] is broken into two sections, (1) the former prophets and histories and (2) the latter twelve prophets. To be clear, the "former" and "latter" distinction is not an assertion of chronology or preeminence, just a description of where they each sit in the Nevi'im (former come first in the Nevi'im, and the latter come second in the Nevi'im). The former prophets and histories are Joshua, Judges, 1&2 Samuel, 1&2 Kings, Isaiah, Jeremiah, and Ezekiel. The latter prophets are Hosea, Joel, Amos, Obadiah, Jonah, Micah, Nahum, Habakkuk, Zephaniah, Haggai, Zechariah, and Malachi. As in the KJV, these books

---

5. *Nevi* is Hebrew for "prophet." In Hebrew, the suffix *'im* is added to masculine nouns to make them plural.

cover a large swath of Israel's history from different angles. The same types of overlap (e.g., Isaiah, Micah, Amos, and Hosea, and 2 Kings) are present here as well. Notably, and in contrast to the KJV, 1 & 2 Chronicles is absent from this collection and is included later. The reason why will be discussed momentarily.

⊹ **THE KETHUVIM**   The Kethuvim, "The Writings,"[6] has three basic sections:

(1) The Books of Truth: Psalms, Proverbs, and Job;

(2) The Five Scrolls (or the Five Megillot):[7] Song of Songs (called the Song of Solomon in the KJV), Ruth, Lamentations, Ecclesiastes, and Esther; and

(3) The narrative texts: Daniel, Ezra, Nehemiah, and 1 & 2 Chronicles.

The Books of Truth (the wisdom texts) function similarly in both Judaism and Christianity. *The Five Scrolls* play a central role in Jewish liturgy during certain holidays: Song of Songs is read during Pesach (Passover); Ruth is read during Shavuot (the Festival of Weeks); Lamentations is read on the Tisha B'Av (the Ninth of Av, which commemorates the destruction of the Temple); Ecclesiastes is read during Sukkot (the Festival of Tabernacles); and Esther is read on Purim. *The narrative texts*, as in Christianity, are just that: narratives.

However, of specific note for this discussion, the Tanakh ends with 1 & 2 Chronicles. This means that the last verse of the last chapter of the Tanakh reads: "Thus saith Cyrus king

---

6. *Kethuv* is Hebrew for "writing." In Hebrew, the suffix *'im* is added to masculine nouns to make them plural.

7. *Megilla* is Hebrew for "scroll." In Hebrew, to pluralize a feminine noun the *a* is removed and the suffix *ot* is added.

of Persia, All the kingdoms of the earth hath the Lord God of heaven given me; and he hath charged me to build him an house in Jerusalem, which is in Judah. Who is there among you of all his people? The Lord his God be with him, and let him go up" (2 Chronicles 36:23). Though the texts which eventually became the Tanakh began to come together during the Babylonian exile (5–6th century BCE), the Tanakh itself was likely compiled in its current form many, many centuries later. By the time the Tanakh, as a book of scripture, came together, the Second Temple had probably been destroyed (that happened in 70 CE), while the Jewish community continued to struggle as subjects of foreign powers. So, concluding the book of holy scripture with a promise of return to and self-rule of ancestral lands, as we see in 2 Chronicles 36:23, is a powerful act of defiance in the face of seemingly overwhelming circumstances and a bold theological expression of hope.

So, what is the story of the Tanakh? What is the overarching narrative? From a bird's eye view, the Tanakh provides a history of God's covenant relationship with the world generally, and also with a specific group of people. The Tanakh serves as the guide to ethics, community, worship and liturgy for those people. And it concludes with a promise of continued covenant keeping on the part of God. The Tanakh tells the story of God's unrelenting and unceasing commitment to Israel and of the requirements, obligations, and blessings that this relationship offers. In meaningful ways, the text, even if cast as history, is intended to be understood in the present tense. The Tanakh suggests that both the requirements associated with the covenant and the certainty of God's commitment to that covenant remain as present now as they have ever been.

My point in going through this admittedly-dense discussion is to foreground a simple reality: When Christians finally strip away the layers and layers of interpretive baggage which have been foisted upon us, and we start to see the Hebrew Bible for what it actually says, we recognize that the Hebrew Bible does not require a Christian gloss to be meaningful, relevant, or understood. The Hebrew Bible (especially when the beauty of the Tanakh's structure is permitted to inform our reading of it) does not understand itself to be incomplete, or in need of additional clarity, or destined for relegation in the face of something new. In fact, it is my strong belief that reading the Hebrew Bible through an expressly Christian lens limits our reading of the text, obstructs our ability to understand the narrative, and closes us off to insight and inspiration. Again, as I noted earlier, I cannot escape my Christian background, and I will account for it as I proceed through the texts, but the reading and analysis of the Hebrew Bible that follows will not rely on or impose a Christianized reading upon it. Rather, much like the overall message which the Tanakh seems to communicate, I will take the text as a present tense expression of God's continued covenant relationship with Israel and the world.

SECTION II

Working with the Text

Just like the last section is not intended as an introduction to the Hebrew Bible, the chapters that follow are not intended to walk someone through the Hebrew Bible book by book or verse by verse. Rather, the chapters that follow are to model or demonstrate some different ways in which the Hebrew Bible might be read, understood, analyzed, and/or examined. The only thing that is common to all of the chapters is a deeply respectful approach which aims to accept the Hebrew Bible on its own terms.

Readers will notice that the subsequent chapters have some variability in the way in which I approach certain parts of scripture or certain topics. In some instances, I am more conversational and take a broader view of a topic with more discussion and less rigor; and in other instances, I am more detailed and specific and dig into topics deeply with carefully footnoted explorations. In some instances, the chapters are longer, carefully crafted arguments, and in other instances the chapters are shorter reflections. I make no attempt to standardize this variability. Rather, this variability simply reflects the different ways in which I have engaged with different topics.

In fact, I see the inclusion of a variety of different types of analysis with different lengths and different approaches to be a feature of this book, not a flaw. The reality is that different people are going to engage with the Hebrew Bible different-ly. And the same person will engage with the Hebrew Bible differently depending on things like how much time one has, what topics are of interest, and what questions one is trying to answer. Through inclusion of various approaches to the text, I hope to reflect that there is not "one way" to read the Hebrew Bible, but rather that we should use what is available to us and go where our interests and the spirit direct. This means that there is no need to read the chapters in this section from first to last. Though reading the chapters in this section in order is certainly an option (and in later chapters I occasion-ally reference material from earlier chapters), readers should also feel comfortable skipping around if that is one's preferred approach. Each chapter is crafted to stand on its own for the most part. That said, there is an order to what will follow. Generally speaking, the chapters are ordered in a way that tracks with the way in which KJV is structured. So, an analysis that focuses on scriptures found in Leviticus will come before an analysis that focuses on scriptures found in Isaiah. Where the analysis is more topical, and not focused on a single book of scripture, I have done my best to situate it based on where the bulk of the scriptural references originate or where the theme makes the most sense, but in some instances that was more art than science.

CHAPTER 4

What to Call the Divine

One of the more interesting features of the Hebrew Bible, and one that is sometimes overlooked by untrained readers, is the various ways in which Hebrew Bible writers label the Divine. Throughout the Hebrew Bible attentive readers will notice a number of different words used for the Divine: God, LORD (all caps), Lord (no caps), and Jehovah, for instance. I think sometimes we skim over these different words, considering them to be synonyms: different ways of expressing the same things. However, other times, and this is something that certainly happens in a Christian context, including in the LDS community, readers try to parse these words looking for meaningful distinctions: Does "God" mean God the Father and "LORD" (in caps) means Jesus? What about Lord (not caps)? Is that God or Jesus, or is it the same term for both? Are the terms completely interchangeable? What about Jehovah? That is obviously Jesus, right?[1]

---

1. The LDS tradition understands God, Jesus, and the Holy Ghost as three distinct beings (a social trinity) and thus this parsing of names may reflect a desire to understand which specific being is discussed in various verses. However, even among Christians who hold a more traditional view of the Trinity, seeking to understand which part of the Godhead is being referenced can be a meaningful exercise.

The goal of this chapter is far less ambitious than some might hope. I am not going to provide definitive answers to these questions. The answers to these questions are really not answerable in an objective sense; rather the answers to these questions are theological claims or statements of faith. For instance, to see Jesus in one or more of these titles one must, at a minimum, (1) presume the Divinity of Jesus and (2) presume that Jesus was in some way known to the writers of the Hebrew Bible. And both of those presumptions are at their core theological claims or statements of faith. The reality is that the way someone answers the questions above says much more about that person's personal beliefs and the camp in which that person pitches their theological tent than it ever will about the Hebrew Bible. Rather, my less-ambitious goal is simply to foreground the different terms that are used for the Divine and to discuss how they are generally translated into English.[2]

El, Adon, YHWH

EL *El* is term for a God or deity that (in its related cognates) was common across all Semitic languages. Back then, *El* functioned much like "God" does today in English: as a general way to describe the Divine (see Genesis 14:18, 19, 20, 22 as one example where this is used). *El* also makes its appearance in a number of names such as Bethel, which means "House of God" and is a combination of *bayith* ("house") and *El* ("God") or Ezekiel, which means something like "God Strengthens" and is a combination of *chazaq* ("to be strong" or "to strengthen")

---

2. This chapter is a surface-level discussion of the names of deity in the Hebrew Bible. The goal here is to introduce the topic, not to provide a thorough treatment of it. There are shades of nuance, complexities, and other ways of naming the Divine that I am intentionally eliding. However, there is a significant amount of scholarship on this topic for those who are interested in diving deeper.

and *El* ("God"). In Hebrew, we find a few variations of *El*; one variation of note is *Eloah*, which is used extensively throughout Job.[3] I mention this one, because the plural of *Eloah* is *Elohim* (in Hebrew, the addition of the *-im* to masculine nouns creates a plural), a name which has particular resonance among the LDS faithful. Like *El*, *Elohim* is a term for God. In the ancient pantheistic religious traditions of some Semitic people *Elohim* was likely a general term that could be used to refer to "the Gods", i.e. the pantheon of Divine beings. Within the context of a monotheistic belief structure that particular term, though grammatically plural, is understood to be a reference to the supreme God.[4] It is *Elohim*, the supreme God, who creates the

---

3. For just a few of many examples see, Job 3:4, 23; 4:9, 17; 11:5, 6, 7.

4. Regarding monotheism in the Hebrew Bible, scholar Benjamin Sommer notes, "The Hebrew Bible provides ample evidence that many Israelites believed in the existence of multiple deities. This is the case for polytheistic Israelites whom biblical prophets criticize for worshipping other gods; but even some authors of the biblical texts seem polytheistic. The Hebrew Bible refers to many heavenly creatures, calling them 'gods' (Gen 6:2; Ps 29:1, Ps 82:6, Ps 86:8, Ps 89:7; Job 1:6), 'angels' (Num 20:16; 2 Sam 24:16; 1 Kgs 13:18; Zech 1:11–12; Ps 78:49; Job 33:23), and 'the assembly of holy ones' (Ps 89:5). . . . [However, if one understands] Monotheism . . . [as] . . . the belief that one supreme being exists whose will is sovereign over all other beings . . . [then there could be] . . . other beings . . . who live in heaven and who are, in the normal course of events, immortal; but they are subservient to the unique supreme being, unless that being voluntarily relinquishes a measure of control. It is not the number of divine beings that matters to monotheism but the relationships between them. A theology in which no one deity has ultimate power over all aspects of the universe is polytheistic (even if that theology knows only one deity); a theology in which one deity has supreme power is monotheistic (even if it knows other heavenly beings). . . . The lower gods or angels of the Hebrew Bible differ from those of Canaanite, Mesopotamian, and Greek literature because they never successfully challenge Yhwh. Many Canaanite, Mesopotamian, and Greek texts narrate conflicts in which a high god is seriously threatened or overthrown. To be sure, biblical texts describe a conflict between Yhwh and the Sea (Isa 27:1, Isa 51:9–11; Hab 3:8; Ps 74:13–15, Ps 89:6-14; and Job 26:5–13). Unlike other texts about fights among gods, though, these passages lack real drama. They convey no sense that Yhwh

Earth and humankind in the first creation narrative (Genesis 1:1–2:3). *El*, *Eloah*, and *Elohim* (and related formulations) are generally translated into English as "God."

ADON *Adon* is a multi-use term that can be used for any person or being who has authority. Like *El*, there are variants of *Adon* throughout the scriptures. In some instances, it is used to describe people. For instance, when Abraham's servant makes a covenant of fidelity to Abraham to find a wife for his son Isaac, the servant refers to Abraham as *Adonaw* ("his master") (Genesis 24:9). However, just a few chapters earlier, Abraham and Lot use this word to welcome angelic visitors, calling them *Adonai*, "my lord" or "my lords" (Genesis 18:3 and 19:2). When *Adon* is used to reference God, it is generally translated into English as "Lord" (no caps). We see this in formulations like *Adone ha-Adonim*, "Lord of Lords" (Deuteronomy 10:17).

YHWH YHWH is sometimes called the Tetragrammaton; it is "the personal name for God."[5] This is a name specific to the Israelite belief system. Out of respect for God's name, it was not pronounced aloud in public. Rather, it could only be spoken by the High Priest on the Day of Atonement (Yom Kippur) and only within the Holy of Holies. This word's original pronunciation is lost to history, but currently most people who choose to articulate it aloud pronounce it as "YAH-way" in English. The name YHWH is prominent in the Hebrew Bible and makes its first appearance in the second creation narrative (Genesis

---

had to engage in real exertion to suppress the insurrection. Baal and Marduk, Zeus and Kronos toil in order to attain an exalted status; Yhwh had that status to begin with and retains it with ease. I stress this point, since without it one could formulate a facile argument that Yhwh is merely another high god like Marduk, Baal, or Zeus." Benjamin Sommer. "Monotheism in the Hebrew Bible." *Bible Odyssey*. https://www.bibleodyssey.org/articles/monotheism-in-the-hebrew-bible/

5. Young, May, "Yahweh." *Bible Odyssey*. https://www.bibleodyssey.org/articles/yahweh/

2:4–3:24). In English, it is most common to translate YHWH as "LORD" (caps). However, there are seven occasions in the KJV where it is translated as "Jehovah" (which I will discuss momentarily). Importantly, in the English translation "LORD" (caps) is exclusively for YHWH.

PUTTING IT TOGETHER This may not seem like much information, but even with this basic background we can start to untangle the Hebrew names for the Divine. Consider Isaiah 1:24: "the Lord, the LORD of hosts . . ." In this verse, the Divine is called (roughly) *ha-adon YHWH tzaba-ot*. Note that *ha-Adon* is translated as "the Lord" (no caps) and YHWH is translated as "LORD" (caps). *Tzaba* is "army/host" and adding the *-ot* makes it plural (because the word is a feminine noun). Hence, *ha-Adon YHWH tzaba-ot* is captured in English as " the Lord, the LORD of hosts . . ."!

Or consider Deuteronomy 10:17: "LORD . . . God of gods, and Lord of lords . . ." In this verse the Divine is called (roughly) *YHWH . . . Elohe ha-Elohim wa-Adonai ha-Adonaim*. Again, YHWH is translated as "LORD" (caps); *Elohe ha-Elohim*, is "God of Gods" (note the singular, *Elohe*; then the plural, *Elohim*); and *Adoni ha-Adonaim* is "Lord of lords (again note singular, *Adoni*; then the note the *-im* at the end of the second *Adon* making it plural—also neither is in caps). Hence, YHWH . . . *Elohe ha-Elohim wa-Adonai ha-Adonaim* is captured in English as "LORD . . . God of gods, and Lord of lords . . ."! With just a little practice, this starts to feel less complicated.

Sometimes it can be hard to know which Hebrew name for God is being used until you look at the underlying Hebrew text. But knowing that in English "God" usually represents *El* (and its variants), and "Lord" usually represents *Adon* (and its variants), and that "LORD" represents YHWH is a really solid start. And taking the time to look at the underlying Hebrew text using an interlinear translation (like the one on bible-hub.com; see my discussion of that in the Annex) is also well worth the time. Aside from being generally interesting, scholars have studied the ways in which the different names for the Divine are used, thereby uncovering patterns of usage that aid in understanding the different strands of tradition that weave their way through the Hebrew Bible. As just one example, and as noted briefly above, *Elohim* is used exclusively in the creation narrative in Genesis 1:1–2:4a. At that point the use of *Elohim* stops completely, and YHWH is used exclusively in the creation narrative in Genesis 2:4b–3:24. This led scholars to the realization that these are really different creation accounts coming from different traditions within the same faith community that were placed side-by-side when the text of the Hebrew Bible was being standardized. Rather than eliminating one account in favor of the other, the redactors of the Hebrew Bible decided to keep both creation accounts, recognizing that each offered meaningful insights. Understanding that these are separate creation accounts makes reading them easier and more instructive.

Jehovah

Now, I want to explore the word *Jehovah*. Again, this is a name for God that has particular resonance within the LDS community. But before we get to that, a little more background is needed. As noted above, the name of God, YHWH, could not be spoken aloud, except at a certain time and place and only by a certain person. So, for verbal readings of scripture that accompanied everyday worship and during regularly occurring religious rites and rituals, it became tradition to substitute *hashem* ("the name") or *Adonai* ("Lord") when one encountered YHWH. Thus, when reading scripture aloud (for instance verses found in Genesis 2) when the reader came upon the name YHWH the reader would say aloud *hashem* or *Adonai* instead of the Divine name.

Further (and this will all connect momentarily), ancient Hebrew was a language that, when written, used only consonants. There were no vowels. To draw some comparisons in English (that do not translate into Hebrew, but which illustrate the point), "God" would be written as "gd" and "Lord" would be written as "lrd." One just had to learn, through context and training, that when one encountered "gd" in the scriptures in which instances it was the word "God" and in which instances it was the word "good;" similarly one just had to learn, through context and training, when one encountered "lrd" in the scriptures in which instances it was the word "Lord" and in which instances it was the word "lurid."

When the Masoretes, a medieval group of Jewish scholars and scribes, were assembling the texts of the Hebrew Bible that are now the standard for our day (called the Masoretic Text),[6] one innovation was the insertion vowel points (basically marks around the consonants) to guide and standardize pronunciation. So, to return to the English comparisons made in the preceding paragraph, "gd" became "g°d" or "g°°d" and "lrd" became "l°rd" or "lᵘrⁱd." As a result of this innovation there was much less potential confusion. But when the Masoretes came across the word *YHWH*, and in an effort to remind readers "do *not* say this name aloud," instead of adding vowels points to aid in the pronunciation of the Tetragrammaton (which was likely impossible anyway, since its original pronunciation had already been lost), the Masoretes inserted vowel points for *Adonai*—that is to say, they inserted *a, o,* and *a* as the vowels for *YHWH*. For those schooled in this effort, this would henceforth serve as a visual reminder: "do not say *YHWH*, but instead say *Adonai*." The result (and I am doing

---

6. See "Jewish Concepts: Masoretic Text" Jewish Virtual Library, maintained by the American-Israeli Cooperative Enterprise, https://www.jewishvirtuallibrary.org/masoretic-text. This work occurred over the span of about 400 years, roughly between the 6th and 10th centuries CE.

this in English, so again it is not perfect but does illustrate the point) is that YHWH was written by the Masorites as Y*a*H*o*W*a*H.

Later Latin-speaking translators simply transliterated the word as it was written. To the Latin-speaking translators, the Hebrew looked like this: J*a*H*o*V*a*H (in Latin J replaces Y, and V replaces W). And so that is how it was transliterated. Hence how we ended up with the word *Jehovah*.[7] This transliteration made its first appearance in English in William Tyndale's translation of the Bible in 1530.[8] *Jehovah* was then carried over into the King James Version just a few decades later (which was completed in 1611, just 80 years after Tyndale's Bible). Today, many do not realize that *Jehovah* is not organic to the original ancient Hebrew Bible texts but instead a transliteration of a Masoretic innovation that was likely never meant to be transliterated in the way in which it was. Despite this reality, in many Christian faith traditions today, it is an unquestioned fact that Jesus *is* Jehovah.

In fact, in some Christian circles Jehovah carries a significant amount of Christological significance. In the LDS Church, Jehovah is considered the name of the "premortal Jesus Christ"[9] and its use in the King James Version of the Bible is cited as proof of Jesus's activity with ancient Israel. Though the name Jehovah only appears in the King James Version of the Hebrew Bible seven times (Genesis 22:14, Exodus 6:3, Exodus 17:15, Judges 6:24, Psalms 83:118, Isaiah 12:2, Isaiah 26:4), common LDS readings generalize this apparent Jehovah-Jesus connection as warrant to understand all references to "LORD" (i.e. YHWH) and "Lord" (since the caps/no caps distinction of-

---

7. Young, May, "Yahweh." *Bible Odyssey.* https://www.bibleodyssey.org/articles/yahweh/

8. "Jehovah." *Etymology Online.* https://www.etymonline.com/word/Jehovah

9. The Church of Jesus Christ of Latter-day Saints, "Jehovah" *Bible Dictionary,* available at https://www.churchofjesuschrist.org/study/scriptures/bd/jehovah

ten goes unrecognized) as potential references to Jesus—in a sense, fully Christianizing Israel's scriptures.[10]

Let me give one concrete example of how this plays out. When Moses attempts to free the Israelites the result is increased brutality upon the Israelites. Moses complains to God about this outcome (see Exodus 5) and, as recorded in the KJV, God replies: "I am the LORD (*YHWH*). And I appeared unto Abraham, unto Isaac, and unto Jacob, by the name of God (*El*) Almighty (*Shaddai*), but by my name Jehovah (*YHWH*) was I not known to them" (Exodus 6:2b–3).[11] But note: the Hebrew name for God that undergirds the KJV's translations "LORD" and "Jehovah" in Exodus 6:2b–3 is exactly the same in Hebrew: in Hebrew, both are *YHWH*. The utilization by the KJV of two different names for the Divine (LORD and Jehovah) is not part of the Hebrew text, but rather a much later Christian construction (which itself is based on a transliteration). Newer, modern translations of these verses simply render both as instances of *YHWH* as "LORD," which is the most accurate trans-

---

10. This plays out most visibly in the chapter headings of the LDS version of the Bible, where Jehovah is used regularly to summarize various chapters despite the fact that the name Jehovah does not appear in those chapter. Also, see for instance Roger R. Keller, "Jesus is Jehovah (*YHWH*): A Study in the Gospels." pp. 120–151. Though Keller acknowledges (in a footnote) that Jehovah was created from applying the vowel points of *Adonai* to *YHWH*, his assertion that Jesus is actually Jehovah (and thus *YHWH*) is almost entirely supported by New Testament texts or New Testament-driven readings of the Hebrew Bible.

11. It is interesting to note that God asserts that Abraham, Isaac, and Jacob did not know the name *YHWH*, despite the fact that the name *YHWH* appears many times before Exodus 6, including in second creation narrative in Genesis and in interactions between the Divine and these three patriarchs which occur throughout Genesis. This claim is likely a remnant of the editing process whereby different ancient traditions were brought together and placed in proximity to each other. In the tradition we see here, Moses was the first to hear the Divine name; in other traditions the name was known much earlier. See Michael D. Coogan (ed), *The New Oxford Annotated Bible*, 4th Edition. p. 86, Footnote at Exodus 3:15.

lation. However, because of the apparent distinction between LORD and Jehovah in the KJV, and because of LDS's adherents somewhat unique beliefs regarding the name Jehovah, LDS readers generally understand Moses to be speaking with a pre-earth Jesus. Yet, when we recognize that in Hebrew text itself no such distinction is made, and when we understand the way in which the name Jehovah came to be, I believe it forces a reconsideration of such claims.

All that to say, in my personal view, premising the re-interpretation of an entire religious tradition based on what was, effectively, a misunderstood transliteration, makes for a weak interpretive foundation and a shaky theological starting point.[12] However, as I noted earlier, assertions like the Jehovah-Jesus connection are not provable (one way or the other) in an objective sense but are rather theological claims or statements of faith.[13] Such claims reveal more about those making them than about what the Hebrew Bible does or does not say. As far as my personal theological claim or statement of faith, I do not need to see Jesus in the Hebrew Bible for the Hebrew Bible to be meaningful for me, nor do I need to see Jesus in the Hebrew Bible in order to have a belief in Jesus.

I Am

Finally, we come to one of the more intriguing names for the Divine: "I Am." Recall that Moses fled Egypt after murdering

---

12. One obvious objection some LDS members might raise is that the use of the name "Jehovah" in restoration texts (like the Pearl of Great Price, Book of Mormon, and Doctrine and Covenants) or in the Temple ceremony is proof that it *really is* Jesus and not a transliteration error. However, my sense is that can be easily rebuffed by simply acknowledging that in the revelatory process, Joseph Smith used the vocabulary that was available to him to express what needed expressing—i.e. the very same logic used to explain the use of the French word *adieu* in the Book of Mormon.
13. Relatedly, referring to Jesus "the Christ" is a theological claim or statement of faith.

an Egyptian. As that story goes, Moses "spied an Egyptian smiting an Hebrew . . . And [Moses] looked this way and that way, and when he saw that there was no man, he slew the Egyptian, and hid him in the sand" (Exodus 2:11–12). When the Pharaoh found out, Moses fled to the hills of Midian where he fell in with some shepherds and became acquainted with Jethro. It is unclear how long Moses was in Midian, but it was long enough to marry Jethro's daughter Zipporah, to have a child named Gershom, and for the "king of Egypt" to die (Exodus 2:21–23).

At some point, Moses was on Mount Horeb (also called Mount Sinai)—called the mountain (*har*) of God (*ha Elohim*)—when an angel of the LORD (an angel [*mal'ak*] of YHWH) called out to him from a burning bush (Exodus 3:1–2). Moses approaches the burning bush, removing his shoes, and God says, "I am the God of thy father, the God of Abraham, the God of Isaac, and the God of Jacob" (all variations of *Eloah*) and calls Moses to lead the Israelites out of Egyptian bondage (see Exodus 3:6–10). Moses, unsure whether the Israelites would respond positively to his claims of a Divine mandate, asks the question, "Behold, when I come unto the children of Israel, and shall say unto them, The God of your fathers hath sent me unto you; and they shall say to me, What is his name? what shall I say unto them?" (Exodus 3:13). Given that Moses was raised outside the Hebrew faith tradition (a fact of which the Israelites would have been aware), knowing God's name would provide Moses needed credibility.

God answers the question thusly: "I Am That I Am . . . Thus shalt thou say unto the children of Israel, I Am hath sent me unto you" (Exodus 3:14). This name, "I Am That I Am" has its roots in the Hebrew verb *hayah*, which is somewhat similar to the English verb "to be" and can suggest things like to be, to become, to exist, to occur, etc. The translation "I Am That I Am" (as appears in the KJV) is not authoritative because the translation itself is difficult. The New Revised Standard

Version (NRSV) renders it "I Am Who I Am." The Jewish Publication Society's translation (JPS) does not even attempt to translate it and just renders the phrase *"Ehyeh-Asher-Ehyeh."* Regardless of the translation, what is apparent is that this is much more than a name. Moses asks for a name (a noun) and God responds by asserting presence and intent (a verb). By any account, this is an ineffable and profound response.[14]

Naming the Divine

As I noted above, my goal in this chapter is not to provide definitive answers to the question about the "right" way to name the Divine. Rather, I only hoped to lay out a few of the most common ways in which the Divine is identified in the Hebrew Bible. The first and most elementary step is the process of connecting Hebrew words with their English counterparts. That is what I have attempted to do here. But that process makes no real assertions of belief. The next step, choosing which name(s) to favor, is where the rubber meets the road. In a very real sense, the name(s) that we, individually or institutionally, use as our labels of choice for the Divine are themselves theological claims.

Through name(s) we assert who the Divine is and how we relate to the Divine. The process of naming the Divine is the very ground upon which theology and faith are constructed. As just one example, "God the Father" and "God the Mother" offer very different theological starting points! Perhaps, now

---

14. Interestingly, according to the Jewish scholar Aruthur Green, there is a connection between Ehyeh-Asher-Ehyeh and YHWH. Green notes that YHWH represents a "grammatically impossible conflation" of the past, present and future tense forms of the verb hayah—all three, past-present-future, smashed together. Green suggests that, in this way, YHWH is tied to *Ehyeh-Asher-Ehyeh*: both are indescribable verbal constructions of hayah. Green suggests that both YHWH and *Ehyeh-Asher-Ehyeh* are probably best understood as something like "I Was/Am/Will Be Who I Was/Am/Will Be. See, Arthur Green. *Seek My Face: A Jewish Mystical Theology,* 2nd ed. pp. 16–18.

armed with a little more information than before, we can each be more intentional about how we name the Divine and be a little more reflective about the theological claims that are inherent in the names of the Divine that we come across in scripture and religious instruction.

CHAPTER 5

Our Relationship with Creation[1]

The Act of Creation

Though it is less obvious in the English translations of the Hebrew Bible, humankind's 'earthiness'—that is to say its interrelationship with creation itself—seems to be a meaningful part of the second Genesis creation narrative.[2] In Genesis 2, God forms creatures "out of the ground" (2:19). In Hebrew "the ground" is *hā'ăḏāmāh*; literally "the" (*hā*) "ground" (*'ăḏāmāh*). As the narrative goes, God created the earth and every plant but observed "there was not a man to till the ground," and so God "watered

---

1. Portions of this chapter, now modified, appeared in various posts on *By Common Consent*: on July 6, 2024 (https://bycommonconsent.com/2024/07/06/relationality-and-creation/); and on Jan 5, 2023 (https://bycommonconsent.com/2023/01/05/the-truth-of-relationship/)

2. For the purposes of this analysis, I am focusing on the creation narrative found in Genesis 2:4–3:24. Generally speaking, as noted in the previous chapter, scholarly consensus is that the book of Genesis contains two creation narratives. Genesis 1:1–2:3 (the *E* creation narrative, using the language of the documentary hypothesis) is thought to have been constructed much later in Israel's history, perhaps as late as the exile. Genesis 2:4–3:24 (the *J* creation narrative) is thought to be a much earlier version with roots back to Israel's origins. In later LDS scripture we see creation narratives that attempt to harmonize the differences between the different Genesis creation accounts. See Anthony Hutchinson, "A Mormon Midrash?: LDS Creation Narratives Reconsidered," *Dialogue*, Vol 21, No 4.

the whole face of the ground" and then "formed man" (2:5–7). The Hebrew word for "man" here is *'āḏām*. This is the origin of the male name (and proper noun) Adam. But in the Hebrew at this point in Genesis, *'āḏām* is not a name or even proper noun; rather, it's a general term that is usually accompanied by the article "the" (*hā*). God forms *hā'āḏām* from *ha'ăḏāmāh*.

The use of the article hā and the obvious etymological connectedness with *'ăḏāmāh* suggests that *hā'āḏām* (likely a play on words in Hebrew) is not a reference to a specific human with a specific name, but rather a reference to a category of creatures. Thus, some suggest that *hā'āḏām* (usually "the human") might be more creatively understood as something closer to "the groundling" or "the earthling."[3] So, in colloquial English, the idea we see in Genesis 2 might be something like: 'God made the earth, and then from the ground God made the groundling.'[4] Though it is true that *'āḏām* is a masculine word in Hebrew, it is also true that the stuff from which *hā'āḏām* is created, *ha'ăḏāmāh* (the ground), is a feminine word in Hebrew. The blending of male and female terms in the creation of the first human creature could be read in a way that suggests that female and male components are co-present, equal parts of human creation.

In fact, it is only later in the narrative where we see the use of different words for male and female, *'îš* and *'iššāh* (Genesis 2:23). This separation between male and female occurs after God takes a "rib" from the side of *hā'āḏām*. Interestingly, the root of the Hebrew word translated as rib, *tsela*, can also refer to the side of a structure, and in some instances a sacred structure (as in Exodus 26:20 or 1 Kings 6:5, where tsela is used for the "side" of the tabernacle or the "side" chambers

---

3. For a solid and extensive discussion on Hebrew etymology in Genesis 2–3 see Ben Spackman's essay, "Adam, Where Art Thou?" in *Fleeing the Garden, Reading Genesis 2–3*.

4. See, for instance, William P. Brown, *A Handbook to Old Testament Exegesis*, 2017 (Westminster John Knox Press: Louisville, KY): p. 257.

of the Temple). Thus, we might think about this part of creation as *hā'ādām* having its "side" removed in order to make a second creature, i.e. the one groundling is divided into two groundlings. Theologically, this view of the narrative communicates that both creatures are made of the same 'stuff' and are co-equal in God's eyes; and architecturally, given where tsela shows up in later Biblical texts, it might suggest certain holiness to this part of creation. As noted above, it only after *hā'ādām* is divided that male and female pronouns are used. Thus, in this creation narrative the initial human creature, *hā'ādām*, is something other than tall, square-jawed white male that is often depicted in LDS art.

Now, let me pause for a moment. For some, the story of a non-gendered groundling that is divided in two to make man and woman may sound a little odd. Despite the fact that this story has been in the Bible as long as there has been a Bible, in the LDS Church we do not often read it this way. But in order to make sense of this story, we need to accept it on its own terms. So, let me be clear about this: the creation narrative in Genesis 2:4–3:24 is not intended as a scientific description of how God created humankind. It is likely not even that concerned with the process of creation (scientific or not). Rather this narrative, and I think many other narratives like this in the Hebrew Bible, is primarily concerned with saying something about God and about humankind's relationship with/to God, with/to each other, and with/to the earth. This is a relationship narrative. Theologian and philosopher Raimon Panikkar might call this a cosmotheandric story—one that connects the universe (*cosmos*), God (*theos*), and humankind (*andros*).[5] Like other mythic narratives, this story primarily

---

5. I borrow this phrase from the theologian and philosopher Raimon Panikkar. As Panikkar explains, this word captures the interconnectedness of the cosmos, God, and humankind. See *The Cosmotheandric Experience, Emerging Religious Consciousness*, 1993 (Orbis Books: Mayknoll, NY).

aims to communicate core values, and a general worldview. It is trying to give us a sense—in this vast universe—of who we are and how we relate to each other, to God, and to the cosmos. And when we see it through this lens, this specific creation story communicates a remarkable message: *Humankind is part of creation. God created the earth, plants, creatures, and groundlings. All creation is made from the same stuff and by the same Creator. And God cares about all of it. God's intention is that humans are to serve the earth and be companions to the creatures. We are all connected and part of one community, under God's lovingkindness.*

Relationality and the LDS Tradition

This view resonates deeply with LDS thinking. One aspect of LDS doctrine which I find particularly compelling is its inclusion of all of creation—humans, earth, animals, etc.—in God's restoration process. LDS scripture states that "all old things shall pass away, and all things shall become new, even the heaven and the earth, and all the fulness thereof, both men and beasts, the fowls of the air, and the fishes of the sea" (D&C 29:24, emphasis added).[6] Echoing the words of John and Isaiah, the Doctrine and Covenants asserts that "there shall be a new heaven and a new earth" (D&C 29:23; Cf Revelation 21:1; Isaiah 65:17, 66:22). D&C 63:21 says that "the earth shall be transfigured," and the 10th Article of Faith makes clear that it is this earth that "will be renewed and receive its paradisiacal glory." Joseph Smith stated God's work includes "salvation of the human family" and also "the renovation of the earth."[7] In

---

6. For a more fulsome discussion of this topic, my essay entitled "A Restoration of All Things." *Public Square Magazine.* June 23, 2021. https://publicsquaremag.org/faith/a-restoration-of-all-things/

7. *Times and Seasons* (Nauvoo, Hancock Co., IL), 2 May 1842, vol. 3, no. 13, pp. 767–782. Accessed via the *Joseph Smith Papers*, https://www.josephsmithpapers.org/paper-summary/times-and-seasons-2-may-1842/10

fact, LDS scripture makes clear that, in fulfilling the measure of its creation, the entire cosmos—the earth, the heavens, humankind, animals, etc. —can be "crowned with glory" (D&C 88:19, 25) and enjoy "eternal felicity" (D&C 77:3).[8] In LDS thought, salvation is a community enterprise and that community includes all of creation. Thus, LDS thought suggests both (1) that all of creation is in relationship with God, and (2) that all of creation is in relationship with each other.

This is also consonant with Jesus's affirmation (which itself reaches back to the Hebrew Bible) that the two great commandments are to love God and love our neighbors as ourselves (Matthew 22:36–40). It is striking that Jesus's summary of "all the law and the prophets" is cast in relational (not pietistic) terms. Consider that in Jesus's Intercessory Prayer rather than a concern that his followers would understand specific doctrinal claims/statements, Jesus prays for a deep covenant relationship. And why? Because covenant relationality is the cornerstone of Jesus's atoning work. Jesus expresses His desire that all of us "may be one; as thou, Father, art in me, and I in thee, that they also may be one in us . . . I in them, and thou in me, that they may be made perfect in one" (John 17:21, 23). Consider the ways the parable of the good Samaritan prioritizes care for each other (i.e. relationship) over institutional or cultural affiliation (Luke 10:25–37), and the ways Jesus's sermon about the goats and the sheep suggests that serving the weak and weary (i.e. relationship) is the essence of a Christian vocation (Matthew 25:31–45, see also Mosiah 2:17). In fact, Jesus teaches that a relationship with Him and with each other is what it means to be exalted. Jesus says this directly, in fact, when he notes that eternal life is "to know . . . the only true God, and Jesus Christ" (John 17:3). In

---

8. This is discussed in additional detail in James E. Talmage's *Jesus the Christ*, chapter 20.

other words, the truth that leads to eternal life is identical to relationality with Jesus and each other.

Paul similarly stresses the importance of relationality. Though not monolithic in his focus, many of Paul's epistles are concerned with relationships within the various Christian communities he served. Indeed, for Paul, unity (i.e. relationality) among Christians is constitutive of Christ's body; that is to say: relationality *within the church* is how relationality *with Jesus* manifests. 1 Corinthians 12 is perhaps the most direct and probably the most sustained articulation of his views on this. Here Paul compares the church to a body with distinct parts that are integrally interrelated and mutually dependent. Additionally, we get a brief description of how this kind of relationality might have looked in Acts, where the people are described manifesting a relationality so complete that they had "one heart and . . . one soul" (Acts 4:32).

The centrality of relationality shows up in LDS scripture as well. The books of Alma, Fourth Nephi, and Moses all point to community as a defining characteristic of what it looks like to live as God intended.[9] In the book of Mosiah, Alma (the elder) teaches that practicing communal care (i.e. relationship) is what it looks like to be God's people.[10] And reinforcing the Doctrine and Covenant's and New Testament's teachings that ordinances are expressly intended to bind people (i.e. create relationships) to each other and to God, President Nelson recently taught, "The covenant path is all about our relationship with God."[11]

---

9. See Alma 1:26–27, 4 Nephi 1:2–3, and Moses 7:18

10. See Mosiah 18:8–10.

11. See D&C 128:9, 18; Galatians 3:29; Ephesians 2:19; 1 Corinthians 12:13–27. See also, Russell M. Nelson, "The Everlasting Covenant." *Liahona.* p. 11.

Relationship and Creation

For reasons that trace back to influences of Greco-Roman thinking on Western Christianity, many Christians, including those in the LDS community, view humanity as 'above' or 'more important than' or 'separate from' the rest creation.[12] Creation is sometimes viewed as little more than a backdrop to a human-centered salvation narrative. Sure, when pressed, we might acknowledge, "of course I need the sun, and of course I am dependent on the water cycle, and of course I take the fruits of the earth into my body to provide nourishment." But even while acknowledging these earthly interconnections in this life, and even while professing a belief that a physical body will accompany eternal progression, we seem to be theologically inattentive to the materiality in which we are enmeshed and generally uninterested in how our relationship to creation might play out in the eternities. Humanity's relationship with creation does not get much airtime in the church meetings in which I have been a part.

The second Genesis story helps correct this error. It teaches us that hā has come from *hā'ăḏāmāh*. When God creates other creatures—every bird, beast, etc. —it is expressly for the purpose of serving as a companion to hā (Gen 2:18–20). It teaches that from hā we now have *'îš* and *'iššāh*, creatures of the same flesh, co-equal, who are to serve and help each other. The second Genesis story also reinforces humankind is to care *hā'ăḏāmāh*. After the man and woman are expelled from the Garden of Eden, they are commanded "to till the ground" from which they were created. (Genesis 3:23). The Hebrew word *ăḇōḏ*, translated in the KJV as "to till" in this verse, can suggest something beyond working the land. It can suggest the notion of serving the land; and in some instances *ăḇōḏ* is even used in the context of religious service and worship. In

---

12. See, for instance, Elizabeth A. Johnson, *Come, Have Breakfast, Meditations on God and the Earth.* pp 159–168.

fact, this idea might be reasonably expressed as being sent forth "to serve the earth," an idea which would match the obvious concern God shows in the earth's creation and of the sense of relationship that hā has with hā'ǎḏāmāh. All this to say, relationality is baked into this creation narrative.

As is the case in all relationality, unless our patterns of behavior are shaped by it, it will never have the power to make us more than we are. For those who profess Jesus, there is a double mandate: that which comes from Genesis and that which comes from the uniquely Christian canon of scripture. Creation, these sacred texts make clear, is our neighbor, with all the responsibility and obligation that entails. What might an increase in relationality with creation look like in the lives of the faithful? This probably varies from person to person, but Catholic theologian Elisabeth A. Johnson offers us some powerful guiding principles: "In place of indifference or spiritual contempt for matter, believers in God become allies with the living God in providential care for all that is created. In place of exclusively anthropological concern, we see that non-human creatures are also worthy of moral consideration. In the face of ecological wastefulness, we name wanton pollution, profligate consumption, and human-induced extinctions as nothing less than grievous sins. [We see] the presence of Christ throughout the natural world."[13]

---

13. Elizabeth A. Johnson, "Jesus and the Cosmos: Soundings in Deep Christology," in *Incarnation, On the Scope and Depth of Christology*, Niels Henrik Gergersen (ed), 2015 (Fortress press: Minneapolis, MN): p. 140.

CHAPTER 6

Imperfect Families[1]

As members of a church that is centered on covenant relationships, particularly those that bind families, it is unsurprising that the stories of Abraham, Isaac, and Jacob loom large in our consciousness when we read the Hebrew Bible. These stories are, at their core, stories of covenant. When viewed collectively, the accounts of Abraham, Sarah, Hagar, Isaac, Rebecca, Jacob, Leah, Bilhah, Rachel, and Zilpah are an uninterrupted narrative about God and God's willingness to reach down directly into the lives of the great patriarchs and matriarchs of the Abrahamic faith tradition. Through these Divine interactions, God forges covenant relationships with people, one by one,[2] as part of God's intention to bless (i.e. to make holy[3]) all of creation. Far from the image of the legalistic and jealous God that some see in the Hebrew Bible, the God of Abraham, Isaac, and Jacob is patient, interactive, engaged, and deeply committed over multiple generations. This is a God who is

1. Portions of this chapter, now modified, appeared in *Public Square Magazine* on March 8, 2022. https://publicsquaremag.org/faith/gospel-fare/imperfect-families-and-covenantal-relationships/
2. See Ronald A. Rasband. "One by One." October 2000 General Conference.
3. *Etymology Online*, entry "bless", accessed 11/29/2024, https://www.etymonline.com/word/bless.

willing to meet these humans where they are and gently lead them into newness.

And it is a good thing God is generous, because the family dynamics that we encounter in these stories are (to say it gently) complicated. Consistent with the "warts and all" approach characteristic of the Hebrew Bible, the families of Abraham, Isaac, and Jacob are portrayed as far from ideal. For example:

- Abraham, at the behest of his wife Sarah, throws Hagar (his other wife) and Ishmael (his son by Hagar) out of his household and into the desert, presumably understanding the great danger this imposed upon them, including a very real risk of dying. (Genesis 16:2–13; 21:9–21)

- Abraham and Isaac, at separate times, both pretend their wives (Sarah and Rebecca, respectively) are their sisters and offer them up to be married to other powerful men and as a way to save their own lives. (Genesis 12:10–20; 20:1–14; 26:1–11 cf. Abraham 2:22–25)

- There is intense conflict between Hagar and Sarah (Abraham's wives) and between Leah, Rachel, Bilhah, and Zilpah (Jacob's wives) when it comes to childbearing and the status it provides - along with painful conflict around the love of Jacob himself. (Genesis 16:5–6; 21:10; 29:30–30:22)

- Rebecca (one of Isaac's wives) and Jacob (one of Isaac's sons) collude to trick an old and nearly-blind Isaac into giving Jacob (who was Rebecca's favorite) the firstborn's blessing despite the fact that it rightfully belongs to Esau. Though they were successful in this subterfuge, Esau is so upset that he threatens to kill Jacob. Jacob then flees to Haran and lives with extended family for two decades. Rebecca recognizes her actions have damaged her relationship with Esau beyond repair. There is no record of Rebecca and Esau ever reconciling. (Genesis 27:1–45)

❧ Reuben (Jacob's oldest son) sleeps with Bilhah, Rachel's servant and his "other mother" (to use language from contemporary polygamous relationships)[4] shortly after Rachel dies in childbirth. (Genesis 35:19–22)

❧ Joseph is sold into slavery by his siblings out of jealousy. (Genesis 37:27–28)

❧ Judah sleeps with his daughter-in-law Tamar, but only because he thought she was a prostitute. (I am not sure if that is better or worse.) She becomes pregnant and gives birth to twins (she also becomes a forbearer of King David, cf. Genesis 38, Matthew 1:1–3).

Perhaps because the LDS community is familiar with, and wants to focus on, the covenant-specific aspects of these stories, we usually jump over the texts that are filled with pain, hurt, duplicity, and selfishness. And yet, I have come to believe that these family stories are just as important as the stories of covenant. Why, you might ask, should we spend time talking about these difficult family stories? The answer seems as obvious as it is profound: because the stories in Genesis are not *only* about covenant making; they are *also* about families. In fact, Genesis makes clear that any discussion about covenant also requires a discussion about the families through which this covenant was transmitted. The two are intertwined. Importantly, the stories of Abraham, Isaac, and Jacob are fully transparent in recognizing that complicated family dynamics are part of life—even for those who seek a covenant relationship with God.

With the ideas clearly in mind that (1) God's covenant and families can be part of everyone's life (even if one is not

---

4. "Glossary of Polygamy." *Deseret News*. June 12, 2006.

married, one comes from a family) and (2) God's covenant and families are deeply interconnected, a beautiful aspect of the family stories in Genesis comes into stark relief: these stories show that God's covenant relationship with humanity continues to move forward even through complicated family environments. We do not need a perfect family to partake in God's covenant. For instance, even while Abraham becomes the father of nations through covenant, the text seems to suggest a fracture in his relationship with his children: though Ishmael and Isaac came together to bury their father (Genesis 25:8–10), there is no record in the Hebrew Bible of Abraham ever speaking again with Ishmael after Ishmael was forced into the desert, nor is there any record of Abraham speaking again with Isaac after the *Akedah* (the Hebrew term for what happened in Moriah in Genesis 22, which translates to "the binding"[5]). Or consider that Jacob, who was heir to the covenant (Genesis 28:10–15; 32:24–30), lived most of his adult life having no contact with his brother Esau (Genesis 31:38; 33:12–17). Though Esau and Jacob have a reconciliation of sorts, Michael Austin points out that Jacob seems content to be freed from the fear of conflict and is not really interested in an enduring relationship.[6] In fact, throughout the Hebrew Bible the Edomites (Esau's offspring Genesis 32:3; 36:1) serve as antagonists to the Israelites (Jacob's offspring). Or despite the fact that Hagar, Bilhah and Zilpah are expressly part of God's covenantal intentions (Genesis 16:7–12; Genesis 49), there was obvious tension introduced through the cultural practice of "giving" one's handmaiden (i.e. enslaved servant) to a husband. Hagar and Sarah (Abraham's wives) and Leah, Bilhah, Rachel, and Zilpah (Jacob's wives) were women who

---

5. Joel S. Kaminsky. "The Akedah in Jewish Tradition." *Bible Odyssey*. https://www.bibleodyssey.org/articles/the-akedah-in-jewish-tradition/
6. Michael Austin, "Esau's Embrace: Thoughts on Genesis 33," By Common Consent, February 27, 2022. Available at: https://bycommonconsent.com/2022/02/27/esaus-embrace-thoughts-on-genesis-33/

might have been, and maybe could have been, friends. But the culture of the day pitted them against each other and created situations rife with exploitation and pain that played itself out through their children. These intrafamily conflicts may have contributed to Joseph's brothers selling him into slavery (Genesis 37:3–4, 11).

Though many of these complicated family situations were not resolved in this life, God's covenantal interactions with these families continued. I realize this is not the way we usually talk about the families of Abraham, Isaac and Jacob, but it is a perspective that is grounded in these Biblical narratives and thus part of our sacred tradition. And as we try to liken these scriptures to ourselves (1 Nephi 19:23), we may be able to recognize some of these same (or other) complicated family dynamics in our own lives or the lives of our friends. In fact, these stories make expressly clear—they even seem to embrace with both arms—the reality that every family has complicated forces at work. Even families of the covenant.

Some families of the covenant have individuals who have effectively been exiled into the desert. Some people may feel like they have been exiled by their families. Some families of the covenant have fractures in relationships among parents/children/siblings; some mixed-marriage families of the covenant are marked by conflicts between the adults, leaving children to struggle with navigating intrafamily relationships; and some families of the covenant have conflicts over inheritance, with certain family members lining up against other family members. The Genesis stories demonstrate that family relationships, even those bound by covenant, may not work out the way we expect; this reality, Genesis suggests, is part of life.

As odd as it may sound, I find deep reserves of hope nestled in the Genesis narratives when it comes to families. I find it comforting that the great patriarchs and matriarchs of our faith—those whose covenant relationships with God serve as the foundational elements of our understanding of God's relationship with humankind and the world—had less-than-perfect families that contained—alongside joy and happiness—moments of conflict, challenge, and discord. They were imperfect, but this did not stop God from interacting with these families! In fact, a central message of these texts seems to be that families of the covenant should expect challenges, but that does not mean that God is not with them. Rather, God persists with these families anyway. God embraces our families as they are—God does not demand (or even expect, it seems) perfect families—and God offers to walk with us as we struggle through complicated relationships. In a culture where anything less than ideal is seen as a failure, the families of Genesis offer us a space for self-acceptance and self-compassion. The family stories of Genesis make clear that God's covenant does not free families from challenges; rather, the family stories of Genesis suggest that God's covenant can persist with us through the very real challenges that will inevitably come to all families.

CHAPTER 7

The Risk of Divine Encounter[1]

When God appeared to Moses on Mount Sinai after the Israelites' escape from Egypt, it was obviously not what the Israelites were expecting. In retrospect, it is easy to understand why. According to the Bible, the Israelites had been under Egyptian rule for about four centuries (Genesis 15:13 and Acts 7:6 say it was 400 years; Exodus 12:40–41 and Galatians 3:17 say 430 years), and for some of that time (scripture never makes it clear how long) they had been enslaved to a Pharaoh who "knew not Joseph" (Exodus 1:8). It is hard to overstate the impact that living in Egypt and being enslaved by Pharaoh probably had on the Israelites. Theologian Walter Bruggeman, borrowing a phrase from social science, describes Egypt's influence as totalizing:[2] the Israelites simply could not conceive of a life outside of the Egyptian culture in which they were enmeshed. In essence, not only were they a people with no way out, but the Israelites *could not even imagine* the idea of "a way out."

---

1. Portions of this chapter, now modified, appeared in *Public Square Magazine* on May 23, 2022. Available at: https://publicsquaremag.org/faith/gospel-fare/embracing-the-risk-of-divine-encounter/
2. See Walter Brueggemann, *The Prophetic Imagination*, 2nd ed., 2001 (Fortress Press: Minneapolis, MN): pp. 1–37; see also Walter Brueggemann, "Preaching the Old Testament." Adapted from a lecture delivered September 2014 at Luther Seminary, Saint Paul, Minn.

And yet, despite being under the thumb of one of the world's great military powers, God introduced the idea of deliverance and demonstrated a divine power that could not be matched—not even by Pharoah. God liberated the Israelites and those that traveled with them (Exodus 12:38) from Egyptian control. There is room for a lively discussion about whether it was 'fair' or even 'right' that all of the people of Egypt suffered under the plagues attributed to God's action (as opposed to just Pharoah), but that is for another day. From the Israelites' vantage point, God proved God's mettle. YHWH was a God to be followed and worshiped.

And so God led them out of Egypt . . . into an unforgiving wilderness, which was another profound struggle. Though freed from physical bondage, the Israelites seem to have had a hard time breaking free from the totalizing influence of Egypt. Creating a new community, based on a new way of being, proved difficult. Their physical situation had changed in a very short time, but their mental, emotional, and spiritual approach to life was a work in progress. More than once, the Israelites bemoaned their situation in the wilderness and openly complained about their liberation, apparently preferring the predictability of bread to eat (even if it meant enslavement) over the unpredictability of following a cloud through the desert (even if it meant God was with them). In hindsight, it is too easy to criticize Israel for this. I am increasingly convinced that our criticism comes quickly precisely because the Israelites' challenges and perspectives hit a little too close to home. In our modern-day wildernesses, many of us would likely trade (or are currently trading) some amount of true freedom for some amount of physical predictability. Despite all of this, God persisted with Israel, and eventually the Israelites arrived at Mount Sinai.

Probably both excited and nervous, Israel prepared to meet God. The One who was more powerful than the most powerful force on Earth would come down and speak directly to the people. But, as I noted at the outset, what Israel got was not what they expected. Exodus says that "that there were thunders and lightnings, and a thick cloud upon the mount, and the voice of the trumpet exceeding loud; so that all the people that was in the camp trembled . . . and the whole mount quaked greatly . . . the voice of the trumpet sounded long, and waxed louder and louder" (Exodus 19:16, 18–19). This was not what the Israelites had signed up for. This was no 'common' deity . . . this was something more. Israel realized in that moment what it meant to encounter YHWH: To encounter this God was to encounter the power of the universe; it was to have your ego stripped away and the frailty of your existence laid bare; it was to come face to face with I Was/Am/Will Be Who I Was/Am/Will Be, whose voice literally shook mountains. And it was too much.

The narrative in Exodus goes on to state: "And all the people saw the thunderings, and the lightnings, and the noise of the trumpet, and the mountain smoking: and when the people saw it, they removed, and stood afar off. And they said unto Moses, Speak thou with us, and we will hear: but let not God speak with us, lest we die" (Exodus 20:18–19). When faced with the opportunity to directly interact with God, the Israelites backed away. In effect, they said, "Moses . . . this is a lot, and it is a little frightening if we are being honest. . . . How 'bout you talk to God and just tell us what he says." Moses tried to convince them that they were ready, that they could do this. Moses is recorded as saying, "Fear not: for God is come to prove you, and that his fear may be before your faces, that ye sin not" (Exodus 20:20). But the Israelites were having none of it. Rather than joining Moses in experiencing the theophany firsthand, "the people stood afar off, and Moses drew near unto the thick darkness where God was" (Exodus 20:21).

Again, I think we too easily criticize the Israelites for their reaction. Many believers, including members of the LDS Church, embrace the notion of encountering God firsthand through the Holy Ghost (and eventually more). We—and I include myself here—tell ourselves that if *we* were back at Mount Sinai, *we* would have stayed to listen. We tell ourselves that we listen to the Spirit in our life now, so we *are* encountering God on a daily basis.

And, of course, there is truth in this. Christian scriptures make it clear that God interacts with creation through the Holy Ghost. But this is false equivalency because that is not what happened on Mount Sinai. God did not say, "come to Mount Sinai where the 'still small voice' will guide you." God said, "come to Mount Sinai to experience Me directly." God was offering to give the Torah (the moral, ethical, legal, and ritual teaching that would turn a group of formerly enslaved people into a holy community) directly to the people of Israel—not simply through the Spirit, but directly; not through whisperings, but by God's own voice. And engaging God directly meant being willing to embrace the ground-shaking, earth-quaking, trumpet-sounding, smoke-billowing, paradigm-shifting experience that came along with it. And this is an entirely different proposition than being open to the Holy Ghost's influence Any criticism we might levee against the Israelites for their hesitancy should be more carefully considered. The fact is that when faced with the reality of God's direct presence the people of Israel seem to have preferred to have a buffer; they seem to have *preferred* to have Moses relay the messages of God. I am not convinced we are that much different.

Something between us and God

This context matters when we read the story of the golden calf. As leaders of the LDS Church (among many others) have pointed out, the story of the golden calf is a story about idolatry.[3] But idolatry in the context of the golden calf story has shades of meaning that we often miss. The kind of idolatry we see in the golden calf story is not really a story of 'worshiping a statue instead of God;' it is a story about wanting to worship God, but also wanting a buffer. It is a story about giving away the option of interacting with God directly. It is a story about focusing on the wrong thing, even though the people believed they were worshiping in the right way. But I am getting ahead of myself. Let us look at the narrative first.

When Moses left the Israelites and walked "into the thick darkness" to talk with God, he was gone for a while. According to Exodus, he was gone for "forty days and forty nights" (Exodus 24:18). Whether it was actually forty days/nights or whether the reference is simply meant to communicate 'a really long time' is beside the point. The central issue is this: after being led out of enslavement and to the base of a mountain that was now quivering under the weight of God's presence, it seemed like Moses, their intrepid leader, had vanished into the mist. This is where a close reading of the text is important to get a sense of what happened next. According to the JPS translation (which I have selected because it is a little clearer than the KJV in this instance):

> When the people saw that Moses was so long in coming down from the mountain, the people gathered against Aaron and said to him, "Come, make us a god who shall go before us, for that fellow Moses—the man who brought us from the land of Egypt—we do not know what has happened to him." . . . and [Aaron] cast in a mold, and made it into a molten calf. And they exclaimed, "This is your god, O Israel, who brought you out of the land of Egypt!" When Aaron saw this, he built an altar

---

3. See, for instance, Spencer W. Kimball's June 1976 article in *Ensign* entitled "The False Gods We Worship." This article is cited in the materials for the 2022 *Come, Follow Me* materials covering the Ten Commandments.

> before it; and Aaron announced: "Tomorrow shall
> be a festival of the LORD!" Early [the] next day,
> the people offered up burnt offerings and brought
> sacrifices of well-being. (Exodus 32:1, 4–6)

What is clear from this text is that the Israelites were not worshiping a golden calf instead of God. That was never the intent; after all, the presence of God was still immediately visible to them on Mount Sinai. They knew the difference between God and the golden calf. And the use of such imagery was not foreign to Israel (e.g., think about the 12 oxen that would eventually support the bronze basin in the temple).[4] In fact, after Aaron constructed the calf they had a "festival of the LORD," and the next day the Israelites "offered up burnt offerings and brought sacrifices of well-being"—all of which was ritually consistent with worship of the LORD. That is to say, every indication is that they continued to believe in and worship the LORD. Rather, the real problem the Israelites seem to be trying to solve in constructing the golden calf was more pedestrian: what should Israel do given that "Moses was so long in coming down from the mountain" and there was no one acting as an intermediary with God?

Recall that prior to Moses ascending Mount Sinai, the Israelites *declined* to experience God's presence directly and preferred for Moses to interact with God and simply relay God's messages to them. But with Moses gone, what was going to happen? Were they going to be forced to interact with God directly? What would that look like? This man, "who brought us forth from the land of Egypt" had disappeared. With Moses absent, the Israelites wanted another buffer, and (pulling from their contemporaneous culture) a golden calf seemed to fit the bill. The golden calf, a common symbol of power,

---

4. For a good summary of bull/calf-related imagery in Israelite worship see Stephen L. Cook. "Bulls in Ancient Israel." *Bible Odyssey*. https://www. bibleodyssey.org/articles/bulls-in-ancient-israel/.

served to represent God to the people. Like Moses, it functioned as a buffer between the people and God. It was a way
to 'safely' have God around without having to experience the
full force of that presence. Thus, Aaron's statement that the
golden calf is "your god, O Israel, who brought you out of the
land of Egypt" is not a misattribution of God's saving power to
an inanimate object; it is Aaron's way of saying, "this golden
calf represents the God who brought you out of Egypt and it
invites God's presence in a safe and manageable way." The
scholar Walter Breuggemann put it this way: "Israel refused
to accept YHWH on YHWH's own terms and distorted YHWH to
make YHWH more compatible to its own needs."[5] The idolatry present in the golden calf story was not worshiping false
gods; the idolatry we see in the golden calf story the desire to
worship a domesticated god from a safe distance, and, in this
instance, through the (mis)use of an intermediary (the golden
calf) that they crafted for themselves.

Understood in this way, idolatry is far more applicable to
modern believers. Discussions in LDS Church meetings that
touch on idolatry generally take as a given that most people
are not literally worshiping false gods—casting this as something only those more benighted people in Biblical times had
done. Instead, we tend to frame the issue more metaphorically and within the context of prioritization: Do we 'prioritize
worldly things' above God (money, status, recreation, etc.)?
This improper prioritization is sometimes termed idolatry.
And because it is probably the case that many folks are doing
OK with regards to prioritization (or at least they think they
are), discussion of idolatry rolls off our backs like water off a
duck. Without discounting that approach entirely, I think the
golden calf narrative points to a different challenge. In Exodus
32, idolatry is not a question of prioritization. Idolatry starts
with allowing, or wanting, or even preferring something to

---

5. Walter Breuggemann, *Deuteronomy*, p. 116.

stand in between us and God. And thus, idolatry, at its heart, is trying to create a situation where we can worship without the risk of direct Divine encounter. Perhaps more often than we realize, idolatry is the human attempt to domesticate God. And this kind of idolatry is far more tempting for modern believers and more prevalent than we might want to admit.

Make no mistake about it, direct Divine encounters can be scary. As noted above, I am not talking about the whisperings of the Holy Ghost gently guiding us along our path. I am talking about something different. I am talking about the kinds of direct encounters we see in the lives of Abraham, Sarah, the Jacobs of the Old Testament and Book of Mormon, Enos, Alma the Younger and the Sons of Mosiah, and Joseph Smith—as well as in the writings of Hildegard von Bingen, Julian of Norwich, and others. I am talking about encounters that are sometimes literally and sometimes metaphorically ground-shaking, earth-quaking, trumpet-sounding, smoke-billowing, paradigm-shifting experiences. These kinds of encounters are risky because, in the end, they demand so much of us. It's not surprising that many of us, and I include myself here, might prefer to avoid this risk. We are content to worship from a distance. We want to worship God, but we also want to do it 'safely.'

How do we moderns do this? In what ways do we create (or allow for) buffers between us and God? I think there are many, ways, but I want to point to a few that may be particular temptations in my own LDS faith tradition. In laying these out, my intent is not to make sweeping, negative generalizations about church worship practices. In fact, as you will see below, all of the things I discuss actually are important, even critical, aspects of our worship life. My point is that we sometimes allow the things that are intended to *support our direct encounter* with God to instead *become a buffer between* us and God. And when that happens—when these things make it so we can worship without the risk of Divine encounter—the story of the golden calf hints that we are potentially straying into a form of idolatry.

⊹ **SCRIPTURES AS IDOL** Many theologians and commentators have discussed the idea of 'Bibliolatry.' This idea suggests that, in some instances, engaging with and defending scriptural texts can become an end in itself. The text, and not the God behind it, becomes the focus of our worship; we become more concerned with the ideal frequency of reading or defending a particular truth claim in the scriptures than whether our study is helping to foster a relationship with God. Sacred texts are critical in that they can help us see the ways in which God interacts with creation But when an encounter with scripture becomes more important than having an encounter with God, we are perhaps engaging in a form of idolatry.

⊹ **CHURCH AS IDOL** The companion to Bibliolatry is 'ecclesiolatry.' The idea here is that, in some instances, membership and participation in church and church-related activities can become ends themselves; we become more concerned with attending church or with our loyalty to church than with how church connects us to God. When this happens, dedication to the church supplants dedication to God, and the actions of church attendance take precedence over the purpose of worship. In my view, and as President Dallin Oaks recently affirmed, the importance of a strong worship community is an indisputable premise—we need a church.[6] The strength of the LDS Church community is one of the defining characteristics of our faith. But when our faith is more strongly centered in a specific

---

6. Dallin H. Oaks. "The Need for a Church." October 2018 General Conference.

organizational construct than in God, or when our engagement in an organization becomes more immediately and emotionally important than our engagement
with God, we are again, perhaps engaging in a form
of idolatry.

✦✦ **LEADERS AS IDOL** Brigham Young once worried that
the LDS community would place "so much confidence
in their leaders . . . [that they would] settle down
in a state of blind self-security, trusting their eternal
destiny in the hands of their leaders with a reckless
confidence that in itself would thwart the purposes of
God in their salvation."[7] A term that might work here
is 'episcopolatry' (if taken in a more general sense of
not referring only to a specific office, the 'episcopy' or
bishop, but to church offices broadly). The fact that
our faith community is guided by inspired men and
women is, I believe, part of why the LDS message resonates with so many people. Keeping in mind the that
the LDS Church embraces the reality that all church
leaders, just like everyone else, are imperfect and
fallible,[8] when our confidence in our leaders (to use

---

7. Brigham Young, *Journal of Discourses*, Vol 27 no. 150. Remarks by President Brigham Young, made in the Tabernacle, Great Salt Lake City, January 12, 1862. Reported by GD Watt.

8. For instance, B.H. Roberts noted: "It is not given to mortal man always
to walk upon that plane where the sunlight of God's inspiration is playing
upon him. . . . Sometimes, the servants of God stand on planes infinitely
lower. . . . Sometimes they speak merely from their human knowledge,
influenced by passions; influenced by the interests of men, and by anger,
and vexation, and all those things that surge in upon the minds of even
servants of God. When they so speak, then that is not Scripture, that is
not the word of God, nor the power of God unto salvation . . .men, even
some of high station in the Church, sometimes speak from merely human
wisdom; or from prejudice or passion; and when they do so, that is not
likely to be the word of God." Roberts, B.H., *Defense of the Faith and the
Saints, Vol I & II,* p. 470. However, for a more recent statement that makes

Brigham Young's terms) becomes 'reckless' and characterized by 'blind self-security'—that is to say, when we forgo direct Divine encounter and cede such things to our leaders—we are potentially engaging in another form of idolatry.

One of the reasons I love the Hebrew Bible is that, even though it is an ancient text, it continues to challenge believers' hearts and minds today. The experience of the Israelites at Mount Sinai is no exception. The story of the golden calf challenges us to consider how, and in what ways, we might be avoiding direct Divine encounter because a more domesticated approach to worship requires less of us. This story challenges us to critically examine our worship lives and consider where we may be giving away the option of interacting with God directly and where we may be focusing on the wrong thing, *even while* trying to worship God. As the story in Exodus makes clear, God *wants* to engage us directly. God is present to us today. Are we willing to ascend the cloud-covered mountain in order to encounter the One whose voice is the voice of thunder and whose presence causes the earth to quake? Are we willing to directly engage the ultimate source of our liberation and freedom? Are we willing to set aside our favorite idols and take the risk of hearing God's voice for ourselves?

---

the same point, see for instance, Nathaniel Givens' 2022 article in *Public Square Magazine* entitled, "The Importance of Prophetic Fallibility."

CHAPTER 8

A Brief Reflection
on Leviticus

Leviticus can feel difficult for modern readers. Though it continues the narrative of Israel's time in the wilderness that begins in Exodus and moves into Numbers, it can be hard to follow. Leviticus recounts important events like the consecration of the priests. Leviticus also describes the dedication of the tabernacle, during which "the glory of the LORD appeared unto all the people . . . and there came a fire out from before the LORD . . . when all the people saw, they shouted, and fell on their faces (Leviticus 9:23–24).[1] But that narrative is also regularly interrupted. In fact, much of Leviticus is direct, detailed guidance from the LORD to Moses (and sometimes Aaron too) regarding how specific rituals should be conducted, various prohibitions that the Israelites must observe, and regulations that Israel and the priests must follow to ensure their holiness. And, frankly, since the LDS community (and Christians generally) often view things like the consecration of the priests, the establishment of the tabernacle, and the observance of the Mosaic laws as an "old" way of doing things, we tend to give

---

1. In Hebrew, the word *kavod*—translated in the KJV as "glory" (as in "the glory of the LORD)—is closely connected to the idea of "presence." So, because God took up residence in the Tabernacle, God's *kavod* (presence or glory) was discernible to the people.

this book of scripture pretty short shrift, believing that it is not relevant for us today (since we have the "new" way). The difficulty of reading Leviticus simply reinforces this view.

In this brief chapter, I am not going to attempt a detailed summary of Leviticus.[2] For anyone looking for a thorough and thoughtful verse-by-verse analysis, I recommend *Leviticus* by Jacob Milgrom (Fortress Press)—it's a really fabulous book. I do, however, want to make a few general, high-level observations which, I think, may demonstrate some ways in which the book of Leviticus is still relevant for modern Christians generally, and for the LDS community specifically.

Observation 1: Doctrine is Policy and Policy is Doctrine

In the modern LDS Church, it is stated with some frequency that church policies might change but the doctrine does not.[3] Implicit in that statement is the idea that policies and doctrines are different things or that the way in which a doctrine is implemented (the policy) is not the same as the doctrine itself. Given that the LDS church is, in meaningful ways, rooted in a Christianity that matured in a society deeply influenced by Greco-Roman thought and noting the LDS church's unique teachings about difference between spiritual and the physical realities,[4] it is unsurprising that a distinction like this—one

---

2. I want to thank Laura for her September 7, 2024 post on By Common Consent, "The Handbook and Leviticus," available at https://bycommonconsent.com/2024/09/07/the-handbook-and-leviticus/, which served as the initial prompt for this reflection.

3. The language distinguishing between policy and doctrine may, in many ways, be unique to the LDS church. For instance, the Catholic church distinguishes between dogma (unchanging truths) and doctrine (which can mature over time), and Protestant traditions, generally, make no such distinction. For LDS discussions on this topic, see, for instance, Dallin H. Oaks, "Introductory Message," April 2022 General Conference, or Glen L. Pace, "Principles and Programs," April 1986 General Conference.

4. Though the LDS church holds that spirit is matter (e.g. D&C 131:7), the notion of a 'spiritual creation' preceding a physical creation' (Moses 3:5)

which seeks to separate the "spirit" of truth from its "bodily" enactment—continues to persist in the LDS tradition. But such a distinction does not exist in Leviticus. In Leviticus, we find embodied doctrine. The rituals and observances described in Leviticus are not policies implementing a more esoteric doctrine; rather, the various rituals and observances are just part of what it looks like to live as an Israelite under the covenant. In Leviticus, doctrine and policy are inseparable because the physical enactment of these rituals and observances is, to use modern language, both doctrine and policy. One lives God's law through embodied doctrine.

I have heard it said that when a society seeks to remember and communicate values to one another and through generations—"values" are, in meaningful ways, similar to religious precepts in this context—these values or precepts are embedded in rituals and observances. That is to say, the values are embodied. And that is exactly what we see in Leviticus. Leviticus is an exercise in the remembering and communicating of values through the medium of embodied doctrine. So, what values do we find in Leviticus? There are many, but a list might include:

- That the people only worship one God;

- That both the people and priests should be holy;

- That God's presence is a discernible reality;

- That purity is both an individual and a community matter, and

- That no matter the situation, there is a way for purity to be secured.

---

and the idea of 'spirit bodies' preceding 'earthly bodies' (e.g. Abraham 3:23) may feed into the notion that a 'spiritual doctrine' is distinct from a 'physical policy.'

These values are embedded into the practices described in Leviticus, and thus they are remembered and communicated over time. Whether it be how sacrifices are to be handled, which religious days are to be recognized, or how priests are to be prepared, through the medium of these practices the values/precepts of the community—the tenets of their faith—are remembered and transmitted. They become embodied doctrine.

Observation 2: Purity is a Community Effort

Both moral impurity, which comes as a result of sin (an impurity of the soul), and ritual impurity, which results from many of the physical aspects of life (an impurity of the body), are directly addressed in Leviticus.[5] I will elaborate on this in a moment, but for now, it is sufficient to observe that Leviticus is concerned with having a people and a community that are pure. Why? It is not because of the promise of a heavenly reward since, at the time of Moses (when the narrative of Leviticus is set) and at the time of the Babylonian exile (when Leviticus probably gained the form we now recognize), the notion of heaven that 21st century Christians take for granted didn't exist. Rather, the concern was much more practical and much more immediate: God's presence was in the tabernacle, and Israel wanted that presence to remain. And impurity of any kind threatened God's continuing presence. To create a somewhat rough example, impurity (both moral and ritual) was like dust that continually settled on the tabernacle; if individuals and the community were vigilant and regularly cleaned off the surfaces where dust gathered by taking the steps to address impurity, then God's presence would remain in the

---

5. The language of moral and ritual impurity, though not used in the Hebrew Bible, is a common way scholars frame the basic categories of impurity. See, for instance, Hyam Maccoby, *Ritual and Morality: The Ritual Purity System and Its Place in Judaism*, 1999 (Cambridge Univ. Press: Cambridge).

tabernacle. However, if the dust was allowed to accumulate, God's presence would eventually depart because it could not remain in a place of impurity.

Of necessity, then, purity was both an individual and community effort. Yes, individuals needed to take steps to address their own moral and ritual impurity. Hence, we find in Leviticus rituals for both priests and non-priests to address the moral impurity introduced by sin, with the priests and non-priests having slightly different requirements (Leviticus 4). And we also find in Leviticus rituals for individuals to address the impurity which comes as a result of normal life, such as menstruation for women (Leviticus 15:19–24) and nocturnal emissions for men (Leviticus 15:16–17). Each individual had a role in preventing the "dust" of impurity from settling on the Tabernacle.

But these individual actions were not sufficient. Leviticus also includes rituals to cleanse the community as a whole, such as the Day of Atonement or Yom Kippur. This day was focused "on the cleaning of the people as a whole and of the tabernacle." The rituals described "provide a means by which the community as a whole could deal with sin's potential communal destructiveness."[6] It is in Leviticus that Israel is given the process whereby a priest, after performing an individual purification ritual, would rid the community as a whole of impurity by laying "both his hands upon the head of the live goat, and confess over him all the iniquities of the children of Israel, and all their transgressions in all their sins, putting them upon the head of the goat, and shall send him away by the hand of a fit man into the wilderness: And the goat shall bear upon him all their iniquities unto a land not inhabited: and he shall let go the goat in the wilderness" (Leviticus 16:21–

---

6. Bruce C. Birch, et al, *A Theological Introduction to the Old Testament*, 2nd Ed, 2005 (Abingdon Press: Nashville, TN): p. 135. See also Leviticus 16:16.

22). This scapegoat, as it came to be known, carried away the community's impurity, thus cleansing the community and the tabernacle, thereby creating the conditions that allowed God's presence to remain.

When it came to addressing impurity, Leviticus makes clear that there was no go-it-alone approach; everyone in the community needed to be involved. The modern-day notion that personal piety and individual righteousness are enough for one's salvation, even if (especially if) the people around you are sinning ("I will be saved, and they will not") is not present in Leviticus. In Leviticus, purity was an individual *and* a community effort. The impure could not just be left behind, because maintaining God's presence required everyone to work together to maintain a communal sense of moral and ritual purity.

Observation 3: Prioritizing Community over Exclusion

I have already hinted at this, but to say it more directly: impurity was an expected part of an Israelite's existence. Even if one could avoid committing sin, things like sex (even among married couples), birth, and death created conditions that led to impurity. Impurity was unavoidable. Certainly, impurity needed to be addressed, but it was also accepted as a reality that impacted everyone. And because impurity was part of life and something that impacted everyone, many of the rituals we find in Leviticus are not about 'penance' (in the Christian sense) but simply a description of how one 'washes off' an impurity that has been introduced. And even in those situations where one had sinned, the focus in Leviticus is about how one becomes clean going forward, not about penance for past actions. Thus, when boiled down to its core, it may be instructive to think of Leviticus as a guide to make sure that each member of the community, and the community as a whole, was pulling in the same direction. Said another way, the ultimate goal of Leviticus is *inclusion*, not *exclusion*. Letting the impure stay impure (morally or ritually) was not good for the individual and it also hurt the community. There is no sense that the "pure" deserve to be part of the community and the "impure" should be excommunicated or cast out. Rather, Leviticus' communal approach to purity recognizes that exclusion of individuals hurts the community and thus there is an imperative to bring the impure back into the community structure. And it was through the embodied doctrine of Leviticus that Israelites enacted that community building.

Implications

I think, once we can get beyond the somewhat foreign language of ritual that we find in Leviticus, it challenges modern LDS readers to consider the objectives of our own worship practices.

First, given what we learn from Leviticus about embodied doctrine, it is worth pondering whether there really is a distinction between Church policy and Church doctrine. If religious practice is simply the embodiment of the doctrine, as Leviticus suggests, then perhaps there is no distinction between the two. Perhaps policy *is* doctrine. To the extent that the policy/doctrine divide has allowed the LDS Church to explain changes in past or current practice that have been harmful, then there may continue to be utility in this framing. But it may also be the case that perpetuating the policy/doctrine divide has prevented us from grappling honestly with our past. Or, thinking about this another way, if it is the case that when a community wants to remember and communicate values, it does so through rituals and observances, through embodied doctrines, what do our past and current rituals and observances, our embodied doctrines, remember and communicate?

Additionally, Leviticus challenges us to think about the way we currently discuss impurity. If it is the case that impurity ought to be addressed on both the individual and community levels, as Leviticus suggests, how might that insight impact our own religious focus? Do we prioritize community purity enough? If not, what does it look like to think about purity at the community level? How might our current liturgical practices be amended or added upon to factor in an increased community focus?

Finally, I am deeply inspired by Leviticus's acceptance of impurity as a part of life. This sort of normalized recognition of impurity not only serves to decrease shame, but to the extent that it is paired with the recognition that overcoming impurity is a group effort; it also creates a powerful scaffolding for community. 21st century Christianity, with its hyper-individualized approach to individual salvation, creates conditions that not only justify exclusion but, on some level, seem to encourage it. But that is miles away from what we find in Leviticus. In the LDS Church, which teaches the principle that "their salvation is necessary and essential to our salvation" (D&C 128:15, emphasis added),[7] perhaps there are ways we can bring Leviticus's community ethos into the modern world?

Yes, it may be true that a book like Leviticus, with its "old" rituals, seems like it might not have much to teach those of us who have "new" rituals. But maybe that is only because we have not taken the time to see what it is really teaching.

---

7. This scripture is specifically talking about "the dead" but the idea can be reasonably extended to include any group of people. This scripture is specifically talking about "the dead" but the idea can be reasonably extended to include any group of people.

CHAPTER 9

Thinking about Tithing[1]

The *Gospel Topic* essay on tithing notes that "the Bible indicates that God's people followed the law of tithing anciently."[2] Similarly, in his May 26, 2022 remarks at the National Press Club, Elder David A. Bednar stated that faithful LDS members live the "commandment of tithing, as described in the Old Testament."[3] These statements, and others like them, may lead some to think that the Hebrew Bible contains a clear, unified description of tithing in ancient times, which, in turn, forms a clear basis for the LDS Church's current approach to this commandment.[4] Though it is indeed true that the principle of tithing is ancient, the descriptions of that principle—in both the Hebrew Bible and in our modern time—are compellingly complex. In fact, there is a surprising multivocality when it comes to descriptions of tithing, anciently and in modern times.

---

1. A version of this chapter originally appeared in *Sunstone Magazine*, "How the Hebrew Bible Might Inform Our Thinking about Tithing," Issue 190, Spring 2023 (40–47).
2. "Tithing," *Gospel Topics*, The Church of Jesus Christ of Latter-day Saints.
3. "An Apostle Describes a Latter-day Work," *Newsroom*, The Church of Jesus Christ of Latter-day Saints, May 26, 2022.
4. See for instance Spencer W. Kimball, "The Law of Tithing," October 1980 General Conference; Dallin H. Oaks, "Tithing," April 1994 General Conference; James E. Faust "The Windows of Heaven," October 1998 General Conference.

In this chapter, I will (1) review how tithing is presented in the first five books of the Hebrew Bible, since these are the foundational texts for Israel's religious requirements.[5] Then I will (2) describe the ways tithing has been implemented in the LDS Church. Let me pause here momentarily to be exceptionally clear: my goal in these first two sections is not to critique or challenge the LDS Church's current approach to tithing. Historical approaches need not dictate how tithing functions today. Rather, the discussion of the Torah's description of tithing and of historical LDS approaches to tithing will set the stage for the last section of this chapter where (3) in the spirit of faithful inquiry, I will consider possible alternative tithing forms that would be consistent with the Hebrew Bible's concepts. Of course, any change to the modern form of tithing would be a matter of prophetic guidance and executed through formal channels.

Tithing in the Hebrew Bible

Tithing is mentioned explicitly in four of the Torah's five books, but its requirements differ in each case.

GENESIS includes two brief references to tithing. Following Abraham's victory over an alliance of regional kings, Abraham gives Melchizedek "tithes of all" (Genesis 14:20). The text does not state what was included in the "all" that Abraham gave,[6] nor does Genesis provide information about Abraham's

---

5. For the purpose of this chapter, I am eliding multiple centuries of Christian and Jewish commentary on tithing-related scriptures. Not only is such commentary outside my narrow scope but also because (1) cataloguing and appropriately analyzing such commentary would require a book-length treatment in its own right (and thus more than I have room for here) and (2) the LDS church does not make an appeal to this commentary when advocating for tithe paying.

6. It is worth noting that Abraham's tithes potentially included the spoils of war. In later biblical text, war spoils were either kept or designated as herem (set apart for destruction). See Charlie Trimm, "Destruction of the

subsequent tithing practices. In the second tithing instance, after Jacob's theophany at Bethel, he vows that "of all that thou [the LORD] shalt give me I will surely give the tenth unto thee" (Genesis 28:22), but we are never informed how Jacob keeps this commitment.

EXODUS makes no reference to tithing.[7]

LEVITICUS says that Israelites should tithe the "seed" and "fruit" of the land (presumably referring to grain, grapes, and olives) and their flocks. Interestingly, when it comes to tithing animals, in Leviticus the Israelites are expressly told not to try to determine the quality of animal given but to simply give "whatsoever passeth under the rod" (Leviticus 27:30–33). These tithes appear to have been given to the Levites,[8] probably to help them subsist, having no land inheritance themselves.

NUMBERS expressly states that tithing goes to the Levites for their consumption, in connection with their temple service.[9] Numbers instructs the Levites to offer a "tenth part of the tithe" as a heave offering to Aaron (and presumably his descendants) and says that the heave offering is "counted unto the Levites" as if it were "the increase of the threshingfloor" and "the increase of the winepress"—hence, in Numbers it seems grain and wine were the only items on which a tithe was required.[10] Though the heave offering was not a tithe per se, the fact of it being a "tenth part" and its textual proximity

Canaanites," *Bible Odyssey*, Society of Biblical Literature. https://www.bibleodyssey.org/passages/related-articles/destruction-of-the-canaanites/

7. However, see the reference to the Sabbatical Year, discussed below.

8. For this discussion, it is not important to distinguish among Levites, priests, or high priests. I will use the more inclusive "Levites" for ease of reference.

9. Other "offerings," including animals, were also given to the Levites, but those were separate from the tithe (See Numbers 18:8–19).

10. For more on the heave offering, see Emil G. Hirsch, "Heave Offering" *Jewish Encyclopedia*, pp. 297–298.

to tithe requirements suggests it could be viewed as connected to the tithe requirement (see Numbers 18:21, 24, 26–31).

DEUTERONOMY'S yearly tithe appears to be limited to grain, wine, and oil (Deuteronomy 12:17; Deuteronomy 14:23). But diverging from both Leviticus and Numbers, the tithe is to be consumed by the household giving the tithe (along with the firstlings of their flocks). The tithe/firstling feast is to be eaten "before the Lord thy God, in the place which he shall choose to place his name there" (i.e. at or near the Sanctuary) as a reminder of God's blessings (Deuteronomy 14:23). Or, if carrying the tithe to the designated feasting location is too difficult, the household is authorized to sell the tithe and take the money to the feast location to purchase "oxen . . . sheep . . . wine . . . strong drink, [or] whatsoever thy soul desireth" and "eat there before the Lord thy God" (Deuteronomy 14:24–26, see also Deuteronomy 26:12–13). Further, during every third year, Israelites pay a "tithe of thine increase" to be used for a feast "within thy gates" (i.e. within their town/community) that is to include not only the household but also Levites, strangers, orphans, and widows (Deuteronomy 14:27–29).

Since planting was prohibited during the Sabbatical Year, every seven years there was no tithe on agricultural goods (Leviticus 25:1–7; Leviticus 26:33–35, see also Exodus 23:10–11).

So, if we are looking just at these foundational texts, this is what we find:

- Genesis describes Abraham's tithe on "all," but gives no indication of how Melchizedek used the tithe—nor whether, or to whom, Abraham offered subsequent tithes. It also does not describe what Jacob's tithes included nor who received them. Notably, tithing is not mentioned before Abraham's time.

- Deuteronomy and Numbers describe tithes that include grain, wine, and oil (or grain, grapes, and olives); Leviticus adds cattle and sheep. However, Leviticus, Numbers, and Deuteronomy make no mention of a tithe requirement for other aspects of a common Israelites' production. For instance, there is no mention of work animals (e.g., donkeys) or birds (some of which were used for rituals) or even other forms of production (e.g., earthenware, textiles, ornamentation, etc.); nor is there any mention of tithing things that might be gathered, like wild fruit, honey, and nuts. In the seventh year, no agricultural tithes were offered.

✦ Genesis never elaborates on the way in which tithes were used. In Numbers and Leviticus, the tithe is used as a means of sustenance for the landless Levites. However, in Deuteronomy, the tithe is used for family and communal celebration.

Thus, it is accurate to say that tithing requirements are described in different forms and for different uses (to the extent that usage is explained at all). Tithing goes back to, but apparently not before, Abraham. Continuing this multivocality on tithing, later biblical accounts continue to present a variety of ways in which the principle of tithing was implemented. Two examples will suffice.

First, the tithe seems to have been connected to royal tributes. Jacob Milgrom, a Jewish scholar and specialist in ancient worship, asserts that the Genesis traditions of Abraham paying tithes to Melchizedek in Salem (later called Jerusalem, the seat of the Kingdom of Judah)[11] and Jacob's promise to pay a tithe to God at Bethel (among Israel's most sacred sites) served to connect tithing with later royal tributes. "The

---

11. Salem is commonly identified with Jerusalem See, Powell, Mark Allan, ed. *HarperCollins Bible Dictionary*. Abridged Edition. San Francisco: HarperOne, 2009. Accessed via "Salem" Bible Odyssey. https://bibleodyssey.org/glossary/salem.

kings controlled the treasure of temple and palace alike," Milgrom writes. Thus "it stands to reason that the tithe, which was originally a religious tribute, came to be channeled to the court."[12] Tithes during kingship translated into a more expansive requirement, which went into royal coffers as a proxy for Levitical support (see 1 Samuel 8:15–17; 1 Kings 15:18; 2 Kings 12:18; 2 Kings 18:15; 2 Chronicles 31:5–21).

However, after the resettlement of Cannan following exile in Babylon, Nehemiah reinstituted tithing (which apparently was not practiced during the Babylonian exile, or it would not have needed to be reinstituted) as part of his efforts to reestablish Israel's worship practices. Israel was operating on scant resources, so, to get the Levites out of the fields and back to the temple, Nehemiah required a tithe, but only on grain, wine, and oil (Nehemiah 13:10–12). It is this same post-exilic period that produced the oft-quoted polemic found in Malachi 3:8–12, "Will a man rob God?", condemning those who do not contribute tithes and offerings. Nehemiah combines the items subject to tithe described in Deuteronomy (grain, wine, and oil) but for the purposes described in Numbers and Leviticus (being given to the Levites to support their temple work).

As noted, these are only two examples of the many ways tithing was implemented in ancient Israel. But these examples reinforce the same conclusion that comes from the discussion of Torah texts above: the Hebrew Bible does not present tithing in a single, consistent way.[13]

---

12. Jacob Milgrom, *Leviticus.* p. 332.

13. In fact, Ezekiel's eschatological vision for a new temple in Jerusalem raises the question of whether a tithe was viewed by all believers as an ongoing necessity. Though Ezekiel's vision of a restored temple includes the reinstitution of a multitude of ritual offerings, "there is no mention whatever of a tithe appointed for the Levites." Joseph Jacobs, M. Seligsohn, Wilhelm Bacher, "Tithe," *Jewish Encyclopedia*, p. 152.

Tithing in the LDS Church Today

Others have provided detailed analyses of the LDS Church's changing approaches to the tithe requirement found in D&C 119.[14] It is sufficient here to note that in the early days of the LDS Church tithing was associated with property and/or net worth, and not with wage earnings. In my view, the transformation to the present day understanding/interpretation of the tithing requirement has its roots in: (1) President Lorenzo Snow's 1899 decree "limiting the law of tithing to one-tenth of annual income with no massive payment upon conversion;"[15] (2) a renewed emphasis and enforcement in 1910 of an 1881 requirement that tithing was obligatory for a temple recommend;[16] and (3) a March 19, 1970, letter from the First Presidency that officially interpreted "interest" to mean "income."[17] These three innovations tied tithing to wages/salaries (versus property/net worth) and established tithing as a requirement for temple access (and, thus, a requirement for exaltation).[18]

---

14. For further reading see: Stephen C. Harper. "The Tithing of My People." *Revelations in Context*; Sam Brunson. "Understanding 'Interest' in Joseph Smith's Original Tithing Revelation." *Juvenile Instructor*; E. Jay Bell, "The Windows of Heaven Revisited: The 1899 Tithing Reformation," *Journal of Mormon History*, pp. 45–83; D. Michael Quinn, *The Mormon Hierarchy, Extensions of Power*, pp.199–204; and Quinn, "LDS Church Finances from the 1830s to the 1990s," *Sunstone*, pp.17–20.

15. D. Michael Quinn, *The Mormon Hierarchy, Extensions of Power*, p. 201.

16. D. Michael Quinn, *The Mormon Hierarchy, Extensions of Power*, p. 202.

17. Though the text of this letter was not publicly released, it was quoted directly by Presiding Bishop Victor L. Brown in April 1974 as part of his response in the "I Have a Question" section of the *Ensign* entitled: "My wife and I want to fully obey the Lord's commandment to pay tithing, but we are confused as to what figure we should base our tithing on. Can you help us?" Available at: https://www.churchofjesuschrist.org/study/ensign/1974/04/i-have-a-question/what-figure-should-we-base-our-tithing-on

18. In the early Church, there are numerous examples of prominent Church leaders not paying, or exempting themselves from, tithing. See Quinn, *Mormon Hierarchy*.

Yet, even today there exist some areas of ambiguity. Robert F. Bohn considered fifteen scenarios where "tithable income" might vary. Though his analysis starts with the (age-old, it seems) debate about "net" versus "gross" income, he goes on to consider situations such as: whether a tithe should be paid on college scholarships, social benefits (such as Medicare, welfare, or Social Security), non-cash income (e.g., in-kind exchanges), gifts/inheritances, or the sale of a home.[19] In most instances, Bohn observes, there are few firm church positions on these (and many other) situations. Rather, it seems, Franklin D. Richards's guidance from 1873 continues to hold true:

> It is not given to the Bishops exactly to tell a man—'You must pay so much.' There is the greatest possible liberality manifested, so as to give every man an opportunity to act upon his own agency in saying what he has made and what he has done with the means which have been placed in his hands, and what he ought to pay as interest or Tithing, so that when the Lord brings these matters to adjudication, we shall be judged out of our own mouths.[20]

The discussion about tithing was reopened for some by a December 2019 leak about the LDS Church having more than a hundred billion dollars in investments, property, and business holdings (this leak was later supported in a February 2020 *Wall Street Journal* article[21]) and by the fine the Securities and Exchange Commission levied against the church and

---

19. Robert F. Bohn. "A Modern Look at Tithable Income." *Sunstone*. pp. 17–24.

20. Quoted in Bohn, "A Modern Look." Discourse by Elder Franklin D. Richards, 28 June 1873, *Journal of Discourses*, 26 Vols. 16:61.

21. Ian Lovett and Rachael Levy. "The Mormon Church Amassed $100 Billion. It Was the Best-Kept Secret in the Investment World." *Wall Street Journal*. February 8, 2020.

its investment arm for improperly obscuring church finances.[22] On one side, some expressed concern that such a wealthy institution would continue to seek financial contributions via tithing; on the other side, some noted that payment of tithing had nothing to do with the LDS Church's financial situation (and of course there were a variety of positions in between).[23] Yet, even in the wake of these disclosures, the LDS Church has remained consistent in its teaching that "tithing is not as much a matter of money as it is a matter of faith"[24] and that "the Church doesn't need [members'] money, but those people need the blessings that come from obeying God's commandments."[25] Currently, the LDS Church's teaching on tithing continues to be that "tithing is the donation of one-tenth of one's income to God's Church . . . all members who have income should pay tithing."[26]

Alternative Approaches?

It seems clear that there are no scriptural, historical, or social requirements tying the LDS Church to a specific method of tithing. Indeed, the opposite seems to be true. In ancient Isra-

---

22. See, for instance, David Michaels and Jonathan Weil, "Church of Jesus Christ of Latter-day Saints, Its Investment Adviser Settle SEC Probe," *Wall Street Journal*. February 21, 2023.

23. These two commentaries capture these positions quite clearly. Jana Reiss, "On Mormon Tithing and a $100 Billion Investment Fund." *Religious News Service*; and Natalie Brown. "Why I Tithe." *By Common Consent*.

24. "Elder Bednar Tells the National Press Club About the Church of Jesus Christ," Newsroom, The Church of Jesus Christ of Latter-day Saints, May 26, 2022. Available at: https://newsroom.churchofjesuschrist.org/article/elder-bednar-national-press-club-summary. Accessed 15 Mar. 2023.

25. "Tithing," *True to the Faith*, 2004, The Church of Jesus Christ of Latter-day Saints. Available at: https://www.churchofjesuschrist.org/study/manual/true-to-the-faith/tithing

26. *General Handbook*, 34.3.1, The Church of Jesus Christ of Latter-day Saints. Available at: https://www.churchofjesuschrist.org/study/manual/general-handbook/34-finances-and-audits. Accessed 15 Mar. 2023.

el and in LDS Church history, tithing has been described and practiced differently. This does not alter the sacred nature of tithing or the requirement to offer tithes. Rather, it is simply the recognition that—as happens in many other areas—the principle of tithing is prophetically interpreted depending on time and circumstances.

With that foundation, I want to end with the following question: Considering that the tithing requirement has been described and implemented differently in the Hebrew Bible, and that the language of D&C 119 has proven to be open to interpretation, how could texts from the ancient scriptural sources change our thinking about tithing? Here are a few possibilities:

- Families could dedicate their tithe (all or some portion of it) for a family celebration/gathering at a temple or other sacred location. This would be consistent with the use of tithes as described in Deuteronomy.

- Only certain portions of "production" could require a tithe (e.g., only a part of one's income, such as income earned beyond immediate family needs, or only interest gained). This would be consistent with Leviticus, Numbers, and Deuteronomy, which presented tithing in one way or another as a tithe on less-than-everything produced and/or gathered.

- Donations to community causes could "count" toward tithing. This would be consistent with the third-year tithe described in Deuteronomy, which funneled tithing resources toward community care.

- Since the LDS Church recognizes that service has a cash value (as is evidenced by its contract with the State of Utah, which places a cash value on service hours[27]), members' church (or community!) service could constitute a portion of tithes as an in-kind donation. This would be consistent with Leviticus's disinterest in whether it was "this" or "that" animal.

⊹ Every seventh year, the LDS Church could observe a Sabbatical Year, where the focus would be on allowing "the land" to "rest." In practice, this could mean making a dedicated effort to contribute to environmental or social concerns, rather than making cash payments to the church.

All the above has firm grounding in the commandment to tithe as described in the Hebrew Bible. And yet, all the above would result in very different experiences and outcomes for the LDS Church, its tithe-paying members, and the surrounding community. As I have already stated, I am not suggesting that the commandment to tithe no longer applies in modern times. Rather, I am simply observing that if tithing is "paid with faith and not money" and if tithing has been implemented in many different ways before, then we as a church have more flexibility than we might realize as we think about how we render unto God what is God's (Mark 12:17; Matthew 22:21).

---

27. Eli Hager. "How has Utah Saved $75 Million on Welfare? By Providing Next to None and Taking Credit for LDS Welfare Instead." *Salt Lake Tribune,* December 2, 2021.

CHAPTER 10

Ancient and
Modern Prophets

Within the LDS Church, we often point to the Hebrew Bible as the basis for our modern-day prophetic tradition. The perspective is often articulated along the lines of, *just as God spoke to prophets like Isaiah and Ezekiel in ancient times, God speaks to prophets in modern times—humankind needs new revelation for its own time and place.*[1] This notion of prophetic continuity is an attractive assertion. The God we encounter in the Hebrew Bible is constantly speaking through chosen servants to communicate with humankind generally, and the people of Israel specifically, within the context of ever-evolving political and social environments. Even with the Christians belief in the unique, revelatory fact of Jesus's Advent, it is hard to imagine that God is suddenly uninterested in the same level of day-to-day engagement that was demonstrated anciently. Certainly, humankind would benefit from God's direct guidance in our

---

1. See, The Church of Jesus Christ of Latter-day Saints, "The Role of Prophets," *Church and Gospel Questions*. Available at: https://www.churchofjesuschrist.org/study/manual/gospel-topics/prophets-questions; see also, Ezra Taft Benson, "Fourteen Fundamentals in Following the Prophet," February 26, 1980, Devotional Address given at Brigham Young University. Available at: https://speeches.byu.edu/talks/ezra-taft-benson/fourteen-fundamentals-following-prophet/

evolving political and social environments. Indeed, it seems obvious to me that, if prophets were useful in the past, prophetic voices would be useful today.

That being said, it is also true that prophets in the Hebrew Bible came to prominence and operated in ways that are quite different from those of modern-day prophets in the LDS Church. In fact, ancient prophetic functions are meaningfully dissimilar from many roles and responsibilities of their modern LDS counterparts. Given that the LDS community has so much invested in the notion of prophetic continuity, including specifically the assertion that the LDS Church is the site of for God's currently chosen and divinely authorized prophetic voice to the world, understanding the ways in which prophets operated anciently seems especially important. After all, if the LDS community's self-understanding is grounded in the reality of prophets, we have a duty to be informed on the topic.

Ancient Prophets

Anciently, prophets could be enigmatic figures. Here are a few examples (and there are many, many others). Shortly after Elijah was carried into heaven in a whirlwind, Elisha, who claimed the prophetic mantle that Elijah left behind, was on his way from Jericho to Bethel. Elisha had just performed a miracle by rejuvenating a spring that had gone dry (2 Kings 2:19–22). As he journeyed down the road, some children made fun of his appearance. The NRSV translates the taunting as "Go away, baldhead! Go away, baldhead!" (2 Kings 22:23). How did Elisha react? According to the KJV: "he turned back, and looked on them, and cursed them in the name of the LORD. And there came forth two she bears out of the wood, and tare forty and two children of them" (2 Kings 2:24). That's right: Elisha used his prophetic prerogative to call bears of the woods to attack the forty-two children who made fun of him.

Isaiah, a prophet deeply connected to the politics of his day, prophesied concerning the events in the town of Ashdod. Ashdod had previously rebelled against Assyria, gaining some degree of independence, and the Assyrians were seeking to subjugate the city. Apparently, the rulers of Ashdod were considering asking the Egyptians (the other large regional power) to support their continued resistance against Assyria. However, bringing in the Egyptians might result in a much larger conflict between Egypt and Assyria, with Israel stuck in the middle. So, Isaiah delivered a message from God about what might happen if Ashdod aligned with Egypt. His message was that "the king of Assyria [would] lead away the Egyptians prisoners, and the Ethiopians captives, young and old, naked and barefoot, even with their buttocks uncovered, to the shame of Egypt" (Isaiah 20:4). That is to say, Assyria would win the battle and all those involved in the conflict, including the Egyptians and any who were aligned with Egypt (e.g., those in Ashdod) would be led into captivity. Aside from the reference to "uncovered buttocks," things might feel pretty standard. However, to drive his point home, and as a symbolic action to accompany his oracle, Isaiah was told by God to walk around Israel naked and barefoot for three years (Isaiah 20:3). Yes: *for three years* Isaiah went around town naked and barefoot.

Jeremiah, the prophet who eventually saw the destruction of Jerusalem, was commanded by the LORD to buy and put on some new underwear. Then the LORD commanded Jeremiah to remove that underwear and "hide it there in a hole of the rock" near the Euphrates River (Jeremiah 13:1–4). (This is already a little odd; God does not, as a standard practice, get involved in the procurement and hiding of underwear.) "After a many days," the LORD commanded Jeremiah to go and retrieve the underwear from the hiding place, only to find that it "was marred, it was profitable for nothing" (Jeremiah 13:6–7); that is to say, because it had been buried in the humid ground the underwear was rotted. The LORD explained to Jeremiah,

"After this manner will I mar the pride of Judah, and the great pride of Jerusalem" (Jeremiah 1:9). So, apparently, Jeremiah's buried and recovered underwear was used by Jeremiah as an object lesson for the people. Presumably, Jeremiah walked around town saying something like, "look at my marred underwear . . . *look at it!*" (holds up underwear). "This is what will happen to your pride."

Ezekiel, at the beginning of his ministry in Babylon and before Jerusalem's fall, was told by God to create a visual representation of Jerusalem under siege. At God's direction, Ezekiel uses a tile and an iron pan (Ezekiel 4:1–3)—those are probably not the materials I would have selected to build a model, but that is what God wanted Ezekiel to use. Then, God tells Ezekiel that he is to symbolically bear the "iniquity of the house of Israel." And how does he do this? By lying on his left side for 390 days, about 13 months (Ezekiel 4:4). When the 390th day concludes, Ezekiel is not done. He must then switch to his right side for an *additional 40 days* in order to "bear the iniquity of the house of Judah" (Ezekiel 4:6).

In a church whose modern prophetic figures look like businessmen—they are almost always seen in well-tailored suits and only available to the public in carefully orchestrated events—ancient prophetic characters like this seem foreign. And in a church in which modern-day prophetic communication is most often done via scripted talks and highly-lawyered messages, these ancient ways of communicating seem outlandish. I have not yet seen a General Conference where the Prophet calls out a she-bear to eat some unruly attendees, or heard of a modern-day Prophet walking around naked for three years to make a point, or seen a talk in which the Prophet holds up some of his destroyed underwear to demonstrate an idea, or witnessed a Prophet lying on his side for more than a year to "bear the iniquity" of the people. The point is that ancient prophets were often disruptive and disorienting figures, and they were critical of both political and religious

leadership. They were not the well-coiffed and highly-pol-
ished elderly gentlemen to which we in the LDS Church have
become accustomed.

Israel's first prophet was Samuel. To LDS ears that sounds
a little odd, I know. It is true that in the Hebrew Bible folks
like Abraham and Moses are labeled as prophets, and in LDS
discourse we talk about them this way. But, as one group of
scholars notes, "that naming is a theological judgment made
by later generations that detected significant continuity between these figures and later prophets."[2] That is to say, the
prophetic designation was *post facto*. The naming of Samuel
as Israel's first prophet is a well-established tradition. In fact,
Peter (Jesus's chief apostle) directly named Samuel as the first
prophet in a sermon at the temple, referencing "all the prophets from Samuel and those that follow" (Acts 3:24). This is not
to say that Abraham and Moses did not communicate with
God—the Hebrew Bible attests that they did, which was part
of the reason they received the *post facto* designation—but
rather it is an acknowledgement that Abraham and Moses did
different things and operated in different ways than later prophetic figures. Where Abraham was responsible for the establishment of the Covenant, and Moses was the vehicle through
which the law was given, those were both unique roles, never
again repeated in the Hebrew Bible.

However, starting with Samuel, and for all the prophets
that followed, prophets served as a "counterbalance" of sorts
to the political and religious elite. Prophets arose alongside
the establishment of the monarchy and the increased cen-
tralization of religious practice. Prophets served to check the
power of the King and to resist the power of those who oversaw the religious structures of the day. Hebrew Bible prophets
were outsiders, not insiders. Many times, they exploded onto

---

2. Bruce C. Birch, Bruce et al, *A Theological Introduction to the Old Testament*, 2nd ed, 2005 (Abingdon Press: Nashville, TN): p. 270.

the stage without warning and just as often disappeared without explanation. As a result of their call and the precarious positions they occupied, they were neither part of the political structure, nor part of the religious structure, and sometimes not even welcomed in the community.

Similarities and Differences

THE DIVINE CALLING   In the modern-day LDS Church, to be ordained an apostle, one must be admitted into the Quorum of the Twelve Apostles.[3] Though the LDS Church's history on this is a little uneven, currently only those who are ordained as apostles are sustained as prophets (they are also sustained as seers and revelators), and the most senior apostle is sustained as *the* Prophet.[4] Only apostles who serve in the First Presidency and Quorum of the Twelve Apostles can select who will join their ranks—this is modeled after what happened in Acts 1 when the remaining eleven apostles selected Mathias to join their ranks. After a selection is made, the selection is to be ratified by a vote of the Church (even if it is a perfunctory vote nowadays). Currently, there is only one capital-P Prophet at a time.

This is simply not how it worked in the Hebrew Bible.

PROPHETS IN THE HEBREW BIBLE   With perhaps the exceptions of Nathan (who seems to have been associated closely with Samuel) and Elisha (who was associated closely with Elijah)—did not receive their call due to their prior experience

---

3. In LDS Church history there have been a few exceptions to this. Joseph Smith and Oliver Cowdry being obvious examples. But there were also folks like Joseph A. Young (one of Brigham Young's sons) and Alvin R. Dyer (who was an Assistant to the Twelve) who were ordained as apostles but were never part of the Quorum.

4. After Joseph Smith's death, there was an initial reticence on the part of the remaining apostles to take the title of "prophet." However, by the 20th century this reticence no longer existed and is now commonly accepted without question.

or previous religious duties or affiliation with a specific person or institution.⁵ Ancient prophets were not selected by existing religious (or prophetic) leadership. And ancient prophets did not require the community to ratify that call. God simply called them, often out of obscurity, and they began their ministry. In fact, one characteristic of many of the Hebrew Bible's prophetic writings is the inclusion of a story about how God called that individual.⁶ Amos, for instance, was a "herdsman" from "Tekoa" and a gatherer of "sycamore fruit"⁷ and then "the LORD took [Amos] as [he] followed the flock, and the LORD said unto [him], Go, prophesy unto my people Israel" (Amos 1:1, 7:14–15). So, Amos went and prophesied. It is unclear where Isaiah was when he received his call. All we know is that he says he saw the LORD enthroned in the heavens, accompanied by six-winged angels, one of whom took a hot coal from the temple's altar and put it on Isaiah's mouth. After this, Isaiah volunteers to carry God's message (Isaiah 6:1–8) and begins his ministry.⁸ Jeremiah's commissioning story is spars-

---

5. I do not include Joshua, Moses's protegee, in this list either since Joshua precedes Samuel and thus precedes the beginning of the prophetic tradition. Also, as I discuss in chapter 16, there are references in the Hebrew Bible to groups akin to a 'prophetic guild.' However there is no textual evidence of which I'm aware that suggests the prophetic guild had any role in selecting/ratifying one who received prophetic call, nor that those in the prophetic guild were more likely to receive a prophetic call than another.

6. John Goldingay observes that these commission narratives often serve a purpose within the larger context of the prophet's message. See "Isaiah's Call," Bible Odyssey, Available at: https://bibleodyssey.com/articles/isaiahs-call/

7. Tekoa is a town outside of Bethlehem. This means that Amos could have been a Judahite, though his lineage is never expressly mentioned. As a herdsman, he was likely wealthy. Amos, who lived in the Southern Kingdom, prophesied in the Northern Kingdom.

8. The Hebrew Bible is silent as to Isaiah's tribal affiliation. Ancient Rabbis suggested that Isaiah was a Judahite, descended from Judah and Tamar. See Sotah 10b. Available at https://www.sefaria.org/sotah.10b

er, simply noting that "the word of the LORD" came to him, and then Jeremiah went to work.[9]

The point is that none of these prophets were selected by anybody other than God; and their selection was not voted on by any person or group of people. God came to and commissioned each of them directly, and, with only the authority of that divine mandate, these prophets began their ministry. The New Testament description of Paul's theophany and his call to the apostleship on the road to Damascus (Acts 9) has much more in common with the Hebrew Bible's description of the prophetic call than does Mathias's selection by the remaining eleven apostles (Acts 1). What's more, in the Hebrew Bible, it was not uncommon for many individuals with prophetic mandates to be operating at the same time (Isaiah, Amos, and Micah all prophesied around the same time, as just one example) and sometimes in close geographic proximity.

RESPONSIBILITIES In the modern LDS church, prophets have increasingly espoused an apolitical stance. This was not always the case; after all, Joseph Smith sought to be President of the United States. From Utah's efforts to be admitted as a state, to the Church's struggles with the U. S. Congress on issues surrounding polygamy, to its stance on political issues like the civil rights movement (which has shifted over the years), the Equal Rights Amendment (which has seemingly not shifted), and California's Proposition 8 (which is largely not talked about now), there is a history of the Church dabbling in political issues of the day, at least in the United States. However, over time, that seems to be diminishing. My sense is that this is partly because the LDS Church is now a worldwide church with members of varying political persuasions, so the desire to be more apolitical is a practical decision that avoids

---

9. Being descended from the "Priests at Anathoth," Jeremiah was likely a Levite.

alienating current and potential members. Also, due to America's tradition of separating church and state, there appears to be a normative reluctance to wade too deeply into politics.

In fact, in the modern LDS Church prophets are best understood as priestly leaders of a large private organization. The modern-day prophet is ultimately responsible for the collection, investment, and expenditure of church funds; he holds the keys to the administration of the saving ordinances; he has the final say on things like how long church meetings last and how youth programs will operate; and the prophet ostensibly approves plans for things like General Conference and other events. Indeed, modern-day prophets are *both* the Senior High Priest and the CEO of an international organization with thousands of full-time employees, millions of volunteers, tens of thousands of buildings, and hundreds of billions of dollars of investments in land, securities, and the private sector. Though, like any leader, the prophet may have more or less involvement in specific aspects of the organization—delegation is key—ultimately, the prophet is responsible for the organization as a whole, its assets, and all those who belong to it. And that is likely a full-time job.

In non-trivial ways, modern-day prophets exercise their priestly authority and carry out their prophetic ministry through the administration of the organization they run. For instance, when Spencer W. Kimball changed the scope of who can be ordained to the priesthood, or when Russell M. Nelson shortened Sunday church service to two hours, or when the temple ceremony was updated, these changes were executed *through* the institution itself. These changes, understood as prophetic acts undertaken by the Senior High Priest, were acts of *institutional governance*. That is to say, modern-day prophets often exercise their priestly authority *via* the organizational structure of the church. In our modern-day world, it is in wielding the power of a massive institution and its assets that modern-day prophets make their mark. Certainly, there are talks, articles, and messages, but ultimately preparing those probably represents a small fraction of the activities the prophet undertakes in a given year and have far less longevity than structural changes to the institution itself.

Again, this is simply not how it worked in the Hebrew Bible. In the Hebrew Bible, prophets were frequently involved in the political affairs of the day. Some prophets, such as Isaiah and Jeremiah, appear to have had direct access to the king and sought to influence decisions on matters like whether to form an alliance with another group, whether to go to war, or whether to capitulate to another regional power's advancing forces. Whether it was Nathan chastising David for taking Bathsheba (discussed in another chapter) or Jeremiah suggesting that the Kingdom of Judah surrender to Babylon (Jeremiah 38:17–23), many of the Hebrew Bible's prophets understood God as acting through history, and thus the politics of the day were fair game when it came to prophetic oracles. And even when they were not involved in specific political decisions, prophets often served to counterbalance Israel's (and later Israel's and Judah's) kings. Prophets were antagonists of royal power, and thus they could be distrustful of the mechanisms of the State.

Furthermore, in the Hebrew Bible, matters of official religious business and leadership of religious structures were *decidedly not* under the prophet's purview: rather it was the priests and high priests—the Levites—who handled such matters. In the Hebrew Bible, even the individuals who might have had these roles at one point (like Ezekiel and Jeremiah) no longer performed those functions once their prophetic call came. Hebrew Bible prophets did not oversee or manage the ways in which believers adhered to their specific religious duties. Neither did they officiate or preside at ritual observances. They did not oversee the collection or distribution of tithes and offerings. And they did not directly oversee the temple or the rites that took place there. Using modern LDS vernacular, Hebrew Bible prophets did not run the Church. They were outside of, and often deeply critical of, the religious institutions of their day. Again, to use modern LDS language, ancient prophets were often antagonistic toward the church. They preached and prophesied and sometimes provided advice to religious leaders, but they had no formal role in religious power structures and sometimes railed against them. Certainly, prophets were vocal about the ways in which religious duties were observed, but they did so from the outside. They were vocal about how resources were used, but they did not oversee the collection or distribution of funds. Rather than figures venerated by millions of devoted believers or senior High Priests over the whole church, Hebrew Bible prophets are often portrayed as somewhat solitary figures who were often on the margins of religious decision making and who may have been disliked by both the religious elite and common Israelites of their day.

SPEAKING FOR GOD Perhaps the single thread that clearly connects the prophets who lead the LDS Church and the prophets we find in the Hebrew Bible is the expectation of their ability to speak for God. And maybe this is the only connection that matters. Both in our modern times and in the Hebrew Bible and, when the person who is the prophet (or prophetess!; see the chapter on Huldah later in this book) opens a proclamation with "Thus saith the Lord" the expectation among believers is that what follows is not the prophet's voice, but God's.

In the Hebrew Bible, prophets do not predict of the future.[10] In fact, the Hebrew Bible expressly condemns consorting with those who offer that service (see, for instance, Exodus 22:18,

---

10. Biblical scholars suggest that those writings which seem to be predictions of the future, e.g. Daniel's interpretation of Nebuchadnezzar's dream of the four kingdoms being destroyed by the stone cut out without hands, found in Daniel 2, were probably written after the historical events occurred and then placed into the text during the editing process. For

Leviticus 19:26, and Deuteronomy 18:10–11). Rather, ancient prophets sought to help reveal God to the people. Sometimes that comes in the form of stark chastisement and sometimes in gentle encouragement. But ancient prophets, in every instance, are seeking to help bridge any gap that might exist between the people and their God. In the modern-day church, this is not terribly different. Modern-day prophets are understood to be God's mouthpiece to the world. And though modern-day prophets do not predict the future, they do seek to communicate God's will.

Extensions and Implications

A reasonable question might be: so, where does that leave us? I can only speak for myself, but my view is that those who believe in a God who continues to call prophets need to be clear-eyed about the differences and similarities between the prophets found in the Hebrew Bible and their modern-day counterparts in the LDS Church. The fact is, in many respects, they are very different. There is nothing inherently wrong with that, but to pretend that Isaiah (for instance) and President Spencer W. Kimball (for instance) played similar roles in society and had similar institutional responsibilities is simply not grounded in fact. Rather, I think we should affirm that prophetic calls look different; different times and different places require different prophets. What's more, I think we also need to be open to the idea that God can call people from various backgrounds to be prophets.

Yes, on the one hand, I mean that different types of people can be called and ordained to be apostles in the LDS Church. But on the other hand, I mean that God may extend a prophetic call outside of the existing LDS Church structure. There is

---

example, Daniel 2's prophecy of the various kingdoms rising and falling likely dates to the 2nd century BCE, well after all of those events happened.

both ancient and modern precedent for this. Numbers 22–24 recount the work of Balaam, a non-Israelite prophet, who was hired by the king of the Moabites and the elders of Midian to curse the coming Israelite army. Balaam, however, is visited by God and instead, at God's behest, blesses the arriving Israelites (much to the consternation of the Moabites and the Midianites!). Balaam was also privileged to see an angel. Despite these remarkable events, Balaam is perhaps most famous for being unkind to his donkey, which ends up speaking to him. But the point is that Balaam was a prophet who was not an Israelite and who seems to have operated outside of the traditional prophetic paradigm of the day. In our modern times, Joseph Smith received a revelation in which God informed him that there are "holy men that ye know not of" but which God has "reserved unto myself" (D&C 49:8). This remarkable statement makes clear that, although Joseph Smith had a key role in the restoration, there were others, unknown to Joseph and the Church, through whom God was working. Taking these two precedents together, I am led to conclude that it can be true both that (1) the senior apostle in the LDS Church is a prophet and "the only person on the earth authorized to exercise all priesthood keys"[11] and that (2) other individuals, not part of the LDS Church structure, can be a prophetic voice for God. I see no doctrinal or practical reason why these truths cannot exist side-by-side.

This view requires that we, the LDS community, make room for a variety of prophetic voices. And, consistent with the Hebrew Bible, it might mean that some of the prophetic voices we hear could be critical of the Church. I recognize that this might be a jarring statement for some. How could a

---

11. The Church of Jesus Christ of Latter-day Saints, "Temple Recommend Interview Questions," *General Handbook*, 26.3.3.1. Available at: https://www.churchofjesuschrist.org/study/manual/general-handbook/26-temple-recommends

prophet be critical of the God-given pattern for covenant keeping? Well, that is *exactly* what Isaiah, and Amos, and Micah, and Jeremiah, and Ezekiel and myriad other prophets did in their times and places. They were not always critical, but they could be. Even more, it may mean that some of the prophetic voices we hear could come from those we may not expect. These voices could be of a different religious background, or they could be female (as just two examples). How could a prophetic voice arise outside of the structure that we believe God has established, a structure that currently requires that a prophet must be both LDS and male? Well, and it is important to always remember this: *God can do what God wants to do.* This does not mean we need to toss out the valuable lessons we learn from the senior apostle in the LDS Church; rather, it means we open the door to receiving additional light and knowledge from additional, non-LDS sources of God's word. This approach places a heavy burden on each of us, individually, to go seek out those who have a prophetic witness. But it may mean we find pearls of great price that we might have otherwise missed.

CHAPTER 11

Lessons from
David and Bathsheba[1]

The story of David and Bathsheba has preoccupied readers of
the Hebrew Bible for centuries. It has all the makings of a Hol-
lywood production, with a narrative that is deeply relatable and
compellingly human. Though the Chronicler seeks to clean up
the story of Solomon's birth by omitting discussion about Uriah and Bathsheba completely (see 1 Chronicles 20), 2 Samuel
11–12 lays out the facts in devastating detail. In many ways, it
is a story of the self-destruction of God's anointed. It is also a
disturbing narrative that explores heavy, painful, and uncomfortable themes—which, in my view, is *exactly why* it belongs in
our sacred text and is worthy of our continued focus.

In my church experience, LDS discussions of the David and
Bathsheba story focus primarily on sexual morality. I don't
think the LDS Church is alone in this approach. The salacious
nature of the affair and the intrigue of the ensuing cover-up—
not to mention modern Christianity's preoccupation with pel-
vic policy—lends itself to seeing the story through this lens.
Whether read as a warning against extra-marital sexual rela-

---

1. Portions of this chapter, now modified, appeared in *Public Square Magazine* on June 11, 2022: https://publicsquaremag.org/faith/gospel-fare/
davids-other-sin-with-bathsheba/

tions, or as a caution against impure thoughts, or as an example of what happens when you are in the wrong place at the wrong time, church lessons of my youth and adulthood taught me (and probably many others) to see David's actions as a violation(s!) of what those in the LDS Church call the Law of Chastity.[2] In fact, the LDS Church's 2022 *Come, Follow Me* lesson material for the section covering this story has this exact focus—it emphasizes and is primarily concerned with David's sexually immoral behavior.[3] It is true that the prophet Nathan understands David's actions as wrong. However, Nathan sees David's actions as wrong for a different reason, and I think this is instructive for all of us. But before we get to Nathan's prophetic response to what David did, let me outline two important facets of the Hebrew Bible that will help contextualize what Nathan says.

First, central to the commands that God gives Israel on Mount Sinai is the requirement to pursue justice (see, for instance, Deuteronomy 16:20). In the multiple ways, and in a variety of different contexts, the Hebrew Bible makes clear that individuals who are part of God's covenant community are not supposed to exploit, take advantage of, cheat, deceive, or mistreat other members of the community (to include the "strangers" who live among them who are not Israelites).[4] Said directly: a life lived according to God's instructions requires *avoiding unjust actions*. Further, God requires that the Israelites proactively care for the disadvantaged (the widows, the orphans, the resident aliens, the poor, etc.) through actions like forgiving loans, providing the necessities of life, redeeming property that had been sold, or freeing Israelites in debt

---

2. "Chastity." *Topics and Questions*. The Church of Jesus Christ of Latter-day Saints.

3. "Thy Kingdom Shall Be Established for Ever." 2022. *Come, Follow Me*, The Church of Jesus Christ of Latter-day Saints

4. Michael Coogan. "Immigrants and Refugees in the Bible." *Bible Odyssey*. https://www.bibleodyssey.org/articles/immigrants-and-refugees-in-the-bible/

bondage. A life lived according to God's instructions requires that members of the community seek to act justly. So, alongside the detailed ritual obligations (like the types of sacrifices to offer and when), the commandments given to Israel outline remarkably powerful social obligations that require the community to take care of each other and to pursue justice.[5] As one good, concrete example, consider Boaz's actions toward Naomi and Ruth (Ruth 1–4). Boaz is one personification of what an ideal covenant-guided life looks like: Boaz both avoids exploiting Naomi and Ruth's situation for his own gain and proactively provides for their well-being, despite the fact that Ruth is from Moab and Boaz had to expend his personal resources to do so.

Second, there are portions of the Hebrew Bible that are rightly categorized as pro-monarchy, and some that even portray God selecting specific individuals to be king. However, the Hebrew Bible is also very wary of kingship. Before the Israelite monarchy is established, in 1 Samuel 8 the priest/prophet Samuel (who preceded Nathan) is explicit about the dangers of having a king, and he lays out a series of dire warnings for what Israel should expect if they choose a king to rule them. Specifically, Samuel warns the people that kings "take."[6] And, according to Samuel, kings do not take of your excess; kings take the things that are foundational to flourishing. Kings take your sons and daughters; kings take your fields, vineyards, olive yards, and seeds; kings take your servants; and kings take the animals that work on your farm as well as the animals you use for food and clothing. In fact, Samuel uses the verb "take" six different times and lists at least eleven different things that

---

5. For a book-length discussion of this topic see Jeremiah Unterman's *Justice for All, How the Jewish Bible Revolutionary Ethics*.
6. The base Hebrew word is *laqach*. For more on this words' meaning and uses see: Bible Hub, *laqach*, https://biblehub.com/hebrew/3947.htm

kings take.[7] According to Samuel, kings often pursue self-interest at the expense of those they are supposed to protect. (As an aside, it is interesting to note how the Book of Mormon, in Mosiah 29, communicates many of the same concerns with kingship as those outlined by Samuel.)

With these backdrops, we can return to Nathan's reaction to David's actions. After Nathan learned that David had taken Bathsheba and tried to cover up his indiscretion, eventually having Uriah killed, Nathan delivered a message from the LORD to David. Here is a version of that exchange which I have somewhat recrafted in more modern language to emphasize the core message (see 2 Samuel 12:1–13):

NATHAN (speaking to David): David, listen to this! There were two men living in the same city; one was wealthy and the other was poor. The rich man had many, many animals . . . multiple flocks and herds in fact. The poor man had nothing except one little ewe lamb. The poor man had raised and cared for this lamb since it was born; the lamb grew up alongside his own children and even ate his food and drank out of his own cup. The poor man loved the lamb so much that it was considered part of the family. Well, one day a traveler came to visit the rich man. The rich man wanted to host the traveler but did not want to use one of his own animals to feed him, so instead he took the poor man's lamb and killed it, and fed it to the traveler.

DAVID (speaking to Nathan): [*With obvious anger and indignation*] As the Lord liveth, the rich man that did this should be put to death! What's more, the rich man should restore the poor man fourfold because of his callous and pitiless actions.

---

7. Yet, even after hearing this, the people said, "we will have a king over us; that we also may be like all the nations; and that our king may judge us, and go out before us, and fight our battles" (1 Samuel 8:19–20).

NATHAN (speaking to David): [*Accusingly*] You *are* the rich man! Thus saith the Lord God of Israel: I anointed you king and I saved you when Saul tried to kill you. I gave you all that Saul had, including his wives. I made you king over all of Israel and Judah . . . and if you had wanted more and asked for it, I would have given it to you. Why, then, did you despise Me and do evil? You had Uriah the Hittite killed with a sword and have taken his wife to be your wife. Because of this, your family will be afflicted with violence and internal strife. You tried to hide what you did, but all of Israel will see what happens to you now.

DAVID (speaking to Nathan): I have sinned against the Lord.

So, what is the lesson here? As noted at the outset, one can derive a lesson in this narrative about the Law of Chastity. Setting aside the question of whether David should have multiple wives and concubines (a topic on which LDS scripture is divided[8]), because Bathsheba was married, David violated prohibitions against adultery. But Nathan's immediate response to David is not a chastity-related chastisement. Instead, God's message for David focuses on David's unjust behavior. On one level, Nathan's parable comments on David's unjust actions by highlighting that David mistreated Uriah. Recall that Uriah was absent for most of the narrative, and thus unable to protect his family. While Uriah was away serving as a soldier in David's army, David "took" Uriah's wife for himself (it is the same verb in Hebrew as the one used in 1 Samuel 8) and there was nothing Uriah could do about it. Even when called back from battle, Uriah's adherence to tradition and his sense of loyalty stands in stark contest to David's deceit (2 Samuel

---

8. In the Book of Mormon the fact of David having multiple wives and concubines is called by God "abominable" (Jacob 2:23–24) whereas the D&C affirms that God gave the multiple wives and concubines to David (D&C 132:38–39).

11:8–13). David's taking of Bathsheba was not because David needed another wife—at this point in David's life it is unclear exactly how many wives and concubines he actually had (see 2 Samuel 3:2–5 and 2 Samuel 5:13), but he certainly had many of them. Rather, David took Bathsheba simply because he wanted Bathsheba for himself. Like the rich man in Nathan's parable, David wanted something that someone else had, and like the rich man, David had the means to take it. So, he did. Thus, this act was a violation of David's obligations as a member of God's covenant community to avoid exploiting those who are in a position of weakness.

On another, and I think deeper level, there is also clearly a lesson about the damage that follows when the powerful (socially, culturally, religiously, economically, politically, and institutionally) fail to protect those who need protection. And, of all the people caught up in this story, Bathsheba is the most vulnerable and the one with the least social power—she is the one who needed the most protection. This is clear in a few ways. For example, Bathsheba is introduced in the narrative as, simply, "a woman" (2 Samuel 11:2), and this nameless woman is cast as a mere object of King David's desire. It is a few verses later, only after David has taken an interest in her, that we learn her name. But even when we learn her name, she is not just "Bathsheba," rather she is Bathsheba "the daughter of Eliam, the wife of Uriah the Hittite" (2 Samuel 11:3). Her identity is not hers alone, but instead she is expressly bound to two different men (this is not unique to Bathsheba; with some rare exceptions, women of that time were little more than property). Further, her marriage to a Hittite (not an Israelite) could have also put her in a position of having less social standing. And, as noted above, because her husband was away she was alone, making her situation more precarious. All of this to say, Bathsheba was not only vulnerable to being exploited, she was also someone in need of affirmative protection. She is like the "little ewe lamb" in Nathan's story; she needed to be proactively protected.

But she was not protected as she should have been. Just as the lamb had no real choice when it was taken by the rich man, when "David sent messengers" to her home (2 Samuel 11:4) there is no indication that Bathsheba had any choice about responding to the King's summons (when the King summons you to his court, you go). Then there was a sexual encounter. Given the vast asymmetry of the relationship—the King of all Israel as compared to the solitary wife of a foreigner who was a foot soldier that was away and serving in the King's army—I do not see any way the encounter between David and Bathsheba could have been consensual, even if no overt force was involved. But, and this is a crushingly painful reality, we have no specific details about how Bathsheba felt about all of this because there is no discussion of the impact of the encounter from Bathsheba's perspective. Like the lamb (who also never has a voice in Nathan's parable and whose view of the actions taken against it are never considered), there is no attempt to consider Bathsheba's feelings about what happened to her. In fact, the aspect of the narrative that most reveals the depth of exploitation inherent in this story is that, after David "lay[s] with her," the narrative makes clear that David was not affected by this affair because "she was purified from her uncleanness" (2 Samuel 11:4). Said another way, the narrative makes sure we all understand *David* did not suffer any ritual impurity as a result of his sexual encounter with Bathsheba because she had bathed herself appropriately prior to being called in to see David (see Leviticus 15:19–28). We are told nothing about Bathsheba's state of mind and no idea how she felt about all of this . . . but don't worry folks, King David is fine!

Thus, Nathan's parable of the rich man and the lamb seems aimed at teaching David that the core of David's sinful activity was that he abused his power both by exploiting those who were vulnerable and by not protecting those he should have been protecting. Nathan helped David see that he had acted toward Uriah and Bathsheba exactly contrary to God's instructions. Uriah, one of David's soldiers, was faithfully serving David. Yet rather than treating Uriah justly, David took advantage of Uriah's absence to take Bathsheba. And Bathsheba, one of David's subjects, was vulnerable due to her husband's absence. Yet rather than providing protection for Bathsheba, David exploited that vulnerability for his own pleasure. David did exactly what Samuel warned the people that a king would do: he took what he wanted in direct contradiction to God's covenant. So, yes, (superficially) this story is about the Law of Chastity.[9] But at its heart this story is really about our responsibility to live justly. And Nathan's initial reaction to David suggests that David's abandonment of justice is the most serious problem.

So how might we apply Nathan's condemnation of 'taking'? Just like in David's time, we live in a world marked by continued and expanding social, cultural, religious, economic, political, and institutional stratification. And too often, those who have the social, cultural, religious, economic, political, and institutional power exploit those who do not (sometimes this exploitation is unintentional, but that does not make it any less damaging). The social, cultural, religious, economic, political, and institutional "kings" too often "take" from those who do not have much to begin with. And just like the Israelites, and just as Nathan taught David, we know that this

---

9. My experience is that when our interpretations of this story focus is chastity then (1) the story is used to justify finger-wagging at those who do not follow this church's chastity standards, and/or (2) the story mostly applies to 'someone else' since those who are in church doing the teaching and the listening do not see themselves as the primary focus of that lesson. In other words, by focusing on the sexual portion of the story it becomes an indirect way to reinforce our own sense of righteousness relative to others' wickedness. If the only lesson we take from a narrative like this is a lesson that primarily applies to someone else, then we are probably missing the point.

"taking" is contrary to God's intention for creation. Rather, the kind of life David should have lived, and the life we have been called to live, is one in which such exploitation does not exist, and inequities are remedied.

Applying these lessons to the LDS Church, we might consider that, in our current world, the LDS Church with its vast financial resources and political influence can reasonably be seen in the role of the rich man in Nathan's narrative—it is an institution with flocks, land, power, and prestige. Does it ever use its institutional power to pursue its own interests at the expense of those who lack the power to resist, or does it leverage its institutional power to shield those with little power from those who would exploit them? Does it ever take from those who have little to begin with, or does it provide for those who are in need, even at the expense of its own self-interests? It is primarily concerned with protecting itself and taking what it needs, or with protecting the vulnerable?

Making this even more personal, many LDS Church members (particularly in industrialized societies) can also be seen in the role of the rich man in Nathan's narrative. Do we use our social or political influence to pursue our own interests at the expense of those who lack the power to resist, or do we use whatever power we might have to shield those with little power from those who would exploit them? Do we ever take from those who have little to begin with, or do we provide for those who are in need, even at the expense of our own self-interests? Are we primarily concerned with protecting ourselves (and our political, social, financial views and interests) and taking what we need, or with protecting the vulnerable?

Once we move beyond superficial chastity-centric discussions, the lesson of this story is one that requires deep and potentially difficult introspection. Are we, as an institution and as a people, acting justly? Are we actively protecting those who are or might be exploited? Perhaps unsurprisingly, this concern with justice has an elevated role in LDS theology. In fact, part of what makes a Zion community—the establishment of which is a primary objective of the LDS tradition —is the presence of *justness* through the *eradication* of exploitation. Consider the description of the Nephites following Jesus's visit: "Every [person] did deal justly one with another. And they had all things common among them; therefore there were not rich and poor, bond and free, but they were all made free, and partakers of the heavenly gift (4 Nephi 1:2–3). Similarly, in the City of Enoch, "they were of one heart and one mind, and dwelt in righteousness; and there was no poor among them" (Moses 7:18). In both of these cases, true covenant-centered living is characterized by a *lack* of exploitation and *proactively correcting* any inequality that may have existed. That is what we are aiming for; and that is exactly what Nathan taught David.

Oh! that we might all live as the prophet Micah said we should: "to do justly, and to love mercy, and to walk humbly with thy God" (Micah 6:8).

CHAPTER 12

Covenant (Singular)[1]

As much as the LDS Church looks back to the Hebrew Bible for things like prophets, temples, and priesthood,[2] there are areas where it clearly diverges from the Hebrew Bible. Some obvious examples include that the LDS Church does not practice the Hebrew Bible's dietary requirements (see Leviticus 11).[3] Likewise, the LDS community does not celebrate the required observances of Passover, the Festival of Weeks, or the Festival of Tabernacles (see Exodus 23 and 34, Leviticus 23, Numbers 28–29, or Deuteronomy 16). A less obvious area of divergence—but one that I think is incredibly important—is the LDS Church's ubiquitous use of the word "covenants" (plural).

The concept of covenant (*berit*, in Hebrew[4]) is, perhaps, the central theme of the Hebrew Bible.[5] In the Hebrew Bible, there

---

1. Portions of this chapter, now modified, appeared in *By Common Consent* on May 30, 2024. Available at: https://bycommonconsent. com/2024/05/30/covenant-singular/

2. To be clear, each of these three things—prophets, temples, and priesthood—look different in the modern LDS church than they do in the Hebrew Bible. Nonetheless, there is a clear intent within the LDS church to establish the general warrant for each of these things within a Hebrew Bible context.

3. Though Doctrine and Covenants 89 strikes a similar chord.

4. "Berit." Jewish Virtual Library. American-Israeli Cooperative Enterprise.

5. For the sake of brevity, and because it is not central to my point, I am skipping a discussion of the relationship between covenant formulations

are five paradigmatic examples of covenant making, which, in meaningful ways, frame much of the Hebrew Bible's narrative and buttress the prophetic instruction that we find in it.

⁘ **THE NOAHIC COVENANT**[6]   As the story goes, before God flooded the earth, God established a covenant (singular) with Noah and his immediate family and with creation (i.e. the animals on the ark) that was quite simple: Noah, his family, and the animals on the ark would live because God remembered them, and they remembered God (Genesis 6 and 7). When the water receded, God (1) extended the covenant (singular) to include Noah's descendants (i.e. all humankind), every creature, and the earth itself, and (2) expanded the covenant from survival to abundant life (Genesis 9).

⁘ **THE ABRAHAMIC COVENANT**   In this narrative, God directed Abram (soon to be renamed Abraham) to

---

in the Hebrew Bible and the Near East's suzerain-vassal covenant formulations. However, I acknowledge that there does seem to be a relationship. For a very, very brief introduction see Adam Lenzi, "How Does the Hebrew Bible Relate to the Ancient Near Eastern World?" *Bible Odyssey*. https://www.bibleodyssey.org/articles/how-does-the-hebrew-bible-relate-to-the-ancient-near-eastern-world/

6. I am not starting with the creation narratives. In my view, the relationship between God and God's creation is clearly implied. Indeed, as Jürgen Moltmann states, "by creating his image on earth, the Creator puts himself in a particular relationship to this being. *Imago Dei*—the image of God—means first of all God's relationship to the human being and then the relation of the human beings, men and women, to God." See *The Coming of God: Christian Eschatology*, p. 72. I think this relationality is further suggested, and in fact extended, when the earth and its denizens participate with God in the creative process (Genesis 1: 11, 12, 20, 21, 24, 25; 2:19–20). Yet even if there is a relationship, some have rightly noted the absence of explicit covenantal formulations in the biblical creation accounts. Indeed, the covenantal formulations that are so clearly present with Noah, Abraham, and Moses, for instance, simply do not exist when it comes to the acts of creation described in Genesis.

leave his father's house, travel to a new land, and accept a new God. Abram does this. In return, God made a covenant (singular) with Abram. In this covenant (singular) God blessed the land, Abram and his posterity, and all the people of the earth (Genesis 12, 15, 17). In return, Abram—now Abraham—accepted God "to be a God unto thee [Abraham], and to thy seed after thee" (Genesis 17:17).[7]

❖ **THE MOSAIC (OR SINAITIC) COVENANT** In this story, when the people of Israel found themselves in bondage to Pharaoh, God heard their cries and remembered the covenant (singular) "to be a God" to Abraham's seed and liberated them (Exodus 2). The Israelites eventually arrived at Mount Sinai[8] and God says that Israel would be a "special treasure" to God, a "holy nation," and a "kingdom of priests" if they would "keep my covenant" (singular) (Exodus 19:5). The covenant to which God referred is the same covenant Abraham made: i.e. that God will be a God unto them, and in return they will be God's people (cf. Exodus 2:24; 6:4–5). *After* the covenant (singular) is articulated and accepted by the Israelites, they are charged with obeying the commandments and teachings Moses delivered (for instance, Exodus 20–23). Despite the debacle of the golden calf, God reaffirmed a commitment to the covenant (singular), and again promised to be Israel's God if they would be God's people (Exodus 34). Again, after God reaffirmed the covenant (singular), God provided instruction.

---

7. Circumcision is the token of the covenant, not the covenant itself (Gen 17:11).
8. Called Mount Horeb in Deuteronomic texts.

✢✢ THE DAVIDIC COVENANT In this story, at the behest of the Israelites, and likely in response to concerns about the growing strength of regional powers, the people of Israel requested that God anoint a king to rule over them. Samuel the prophet anointed the Benjamite Saul to be king (see 1 Samuel 8:4–22, 10:17–24). Following Saul's demise, Samuel anointed the Judahite David to be king. Though God prevents David from building a temple, God promised him, "I will establish [your] kingdom . . . and [your] house and [your] kingdom shall be enshrined forever before thee; thy throne shall be established for ever" (see, 2 Sa, 7 12–14, 16). Going forward, Israel considers the Davidic line to be the mechanism through which God will bring peace to the land and prosperity to the people of the world (see the chapter entitled "On Reading Isaiah" for additional discussion on this point).

✢✢ THE TEMPLE COVENANT / INVIOLABILITY OF JERUSALEM This one is a little different than the preceding four, but I think it is important enough to be mentioned alongside them. According to the narrative, when the Israelites finished constructing Solomon's Temple, the Ark of the Covenant was installed in the Holy of Holies. (Since the time of Israel's journeyings in the wilderness, the Ark served as a physical reminder of God's presence—the winged seraphs atop the Ark were God's footstool.) With the Ark in place, the presence of God filled the temple. Solomon spoke to the people and stated that the temple would serve as "a settled place for [God] to abide for ever (See 1 Kings 8:3–13). Shortly thereafter, God spoke to Solomon and affirmed, "I have hallowed this house, which thou hast built, to put my name there for ever; and mine eyes and mine heart shall be there perpetually.

And if thou wilt walk before me . . . in integrity of heart, and in uprightness, to do according to all that I have commanded thee, and wilt keep my statutes and my judgments then I will establish the throne of thy kingdom upon Israel for ever, as I promised to David thy father, saying, There shall not fail thee a man upon the throne of Israel (1 Kings 9:3b–4). From thenceforth, Jerusalem, and specifically the temple, was the center of God's presence in the world and the emanation point for all of God's redeeming work (Isaiah 56:7; Ezekiel 56:5).

It is worth pausing momentarily to reflect upon the similarities of these five covenant (singular) formulations. If one simultaneously looks at them closely and considers them broadly, it becomes clear that they are, functionally, rearticulations of the same foundational covenant:

- they all establish a relationship of mutual affection and trust;

- they are all radically inclusive, affirming lovingkindness for *both* a specific person/group of people *as well as* all the people of the earth;

- they all recognize the sacredness (i.e. the consecratedness) of a specific place or the earth more generally; and

- they are all expressions of God's fidelity to all that God created.

In sum: these are not five separate *covenants* (plural); rather, they are variations on the same *covenant* (singular): a covenant that articulates a loving and caring relationship among God, humankind, and creation.

I am happy to be corrected on this, but I have found no instance in Hebrew Bible of the use of the word *covenants* (plural)[9] to describe the reality of a relationship between God, God's people, and creation. Rather, in the Hebrew Bible *covenant* (singular) is used, over and over, to describe this relationship. Certainly, there are requirements and obligations that accompany the relationship (as is made clear in Exodus 19, for instance). Yes, these requirements and obligations are what it looks like to be in—are the embodiment of—a covenant relationship with God, but they *are not the covenant itself.* The covenant (singular) remains, at its core, "I am your God" and "we are God's people." Despite the fact that Israel fails to follow these requirements and obligations, time and time again it is the fact and force of God's covenant (singular) with Israel that moves God to action (see, for instance, Exodus 3, Hosea 2, Ezekiel 16, and Isaiah 59).

Notably, Jesus references and carries forward the same focus on covenant (singular). The King James Version's translation of the synoptic gospels' description of the Last Supper all record Jesus affirming a new "testament" as he passes around the cup of wine (Matthew 26, Luke 22, Mark 14). The underlying Greek word, *diathéké*, is present sixteen other times in the New Testament and is generally translated as "covenant"—in fact, many other English Bible translations use "covenant" instead of "testament" in their renderings of Jesus's language in the above scriptural texts. The vast majority of the time in the New Testament *diathéké* (covenant) is singular, including Jesus's use of the word at the Last Supper.[10]

And, yet, somewhere along the way—and there are probably Christian historians who know how this happened, but I'm

---

9. By this I mean a plural version of the Hebrew word *berit*. As an aside, in LDS scriptures the "covenants" (plural) is used occasionally in the Hebrew Bible's chapter headings, but, obviously, those are not original to the text.
10. There are three instances where the word is plural: Roman 9:4, Galatians 4:24 (both *diathēkai*), and Ephesians 2:12 (*diathēkōn*). However, the use of "covenants" (plural) is ubiquitous in the Book of Mormon, which uses "covenants" far more than any other book of LDS scripture.

not one of them—the word covenant became a synonym for contract, even though they mean very different things. Where a covenant is premised on trust, a contract is premised on mistrust; where a covenant is focused on relationships, a contract is focused on transactions. Covenant, by its very nature, is expressly centered on relationality and is an expression of mercy, love, and devotion. Contracts, by their very nature, are expressly centered on the other party's obligations and responsibilities, and outline terms of a wholly conditional engagement. Where a covenant is "I am yours and you are mine, forever" a contract is "I'll do this *but only* if you do the following things, and, even then, *only* for the time specified."[11] That is to say, we started saying *covenants* (plural) and we began thinking in terms of contract. And when this happened, we lost the notion of *covenant* (singular).

⁘ We stopped using the word *covenant* (singular) to describe the sweeping relationship between God, God's people, and creation; and instead, we started using the word *covenants* (plural) to describe narrowly focused, hyper-individualized interactions with a book-keeper God that is primarily (and mostly) attentive to acts of private orthodoxy.

---

11. Though not explored here, some LDS thinkers and teachers' views of 'the fall' may reinforce this contract-centric view of covenants (plural). If humans are sinful and unfaithful as a result of 'the fall'—as LDS teaching suggests—then mistrust and conditional love on God's part may be warranted (see Russel M. Nelson, "Divine Love," https://www.churchofjesus-christ.org/study/ensign/2003/02 for a discussion of the apparently-conditional nature of God's love). However, as the scholar Terence Fretheim notes, the Christian doctrine of 'the fall' does not have its origin in the Hebrew Bible Despite the fact that Christians cite Hebrew Bible texts to support the doctrine, the doctrine of 'the fall' has been "mediated to us through Augustine, the reformers, and others"—i.e. the doctrine of 'the fall' is a Christianized reading of the Hebrew Bible and not explicit in the Hebrew Bible itself. See Terence E. Fretheim, "Is Genesis 3 a Fall Story?," *Word and World*, pp. 144–53.

⁍ *Covenant* (singular), which used to describe a continuing cosmic connection, morphed into *covenants* (plural), which now describes an entirely contingent contract.

⁍ To "remember and keep the covenant (singular)" used to be a community exercise of recalling a creation-aware relationship anchored in trust, that "God is our God, and we are God's people," regardless of all other realities. Nowadays, "remembering and keeping our covenants (plural)" is a creation-agnostic, exercise of accounting for personal performance relative to a specific set of obligations and responsibilities, and always within the horizon of retribution or reward.

⁍ The word *covenant* (singular) is used to invoke the idea of a singular relationship between God, God's people, and creation that was an indisputable and immutable fact—a fact that precedes responsibilities and obligations. Nowadays, *covenants* (plural) invokes the idea of a deeply transactional and conditional arrangement.

To be clear, I know that the LDS Church is not alone in this shift. Other Christian denominations have embraced a contract-based perspective on the relationship with the Divine. But I admit to longing for the ancient view of covenant (singular) to reemerge in our collective LDS consciousness. And, to be exceptionally clear about this, such a view is squarely within the theological horizon of LDS doctrine in LDS scripture God's covenant (singular) with Israel is continually expanding physically and temporally—following different groups as they settle different lands and persisting in these new lands through countless generations. Furthermore, in LDS scripture, the Restoration is expressly linked back to, and seen as directly connected with, the people (e.g., Abraham) and places (e.g., temples) through which God's covenant (singular) with Israel was made real and tangible.[12] For the LDS Church, re-embracing the ancient view of covenant (singular) would certainly require a change to the way it talks and thinks about covenant (singular)—specifically, it would need to jettison the covenants (plural)/contract framing—but such a change is one that the LDS Church's sacred text fully supports that and, I believe, more faithful to the ancient faith tradition to which the LDS Church says it is connected.

More personally, this ancient view of covenant (singular) It is what speaks to me most powerfully. I know I do not, and really cannot, keep all of the obligations and responsibilities that God has laid out for me. So, to use modern language, I do not "remember and keep my covenants (plural)" as well as I ought. But God is my God. And I want to be one with and one of God's people. I know that, before all other things, I am bound in a cosmic relationship with God, and with everyone and everything around me. I want to live in a way that is guided by this reality. That is to say, I can "remember to keep this covenant" (singular), and this covenant (singular) continues to anchor me.

---

12. For a much more thorough discussion of the ways in which LDS teaching separates itself from Reformed covenant theology see Terryl Givens, *Wrestling the Angel*, pp. 176–180.

CHAPTER 13

Huldah, The Prophetess

We know tantalizingly little about Huldah. In the Hebrew Bible, she surfaces in a single story, recounted (with some variation) in both 2 Kings 22 and 2 Chronicles 34. And yet, the role she plays in this single story is remarkable. But before getting to Huldah, it is worth spending a little time setting up the context.

The Backdrop

Around 640 BCE, following the assassination of his father, Amon, Josiah became king of the Southern Kingdom of Judah. According to the text, he was eight years old when this happened. He was the grandson of Manasseh, an infamously wicked king (2 Kings 2:9–20), and the great-grandson of Hezekiah (whose birth Isaiah was likely anticipating in Isaiah 9). Josiah ascended to his throne at an interesting time. Since the time of the Assyrian invasion of the Northern Kingdom 100 years earlier, Judah had been a vassal state of the Assyrian empire. As time passed, and as powerful Assyrian leaders died, the Assyrian grip on Judah began to slip. Egypt, the other regional power, was in a similarly weak position, and so the Kingdom of Judah had, for the first time in a long time, some degree of autonomy.

When he was about 26 years old, in the 18th year of his reign, Josiah took advantage of this relative autonomy and began a reform effort in the Kingdom of Judah. According to the Hebrew Bible narrative, this effort was driven by a sense of religious devotion: Josiah sought to restore a focus on God and the temple that had, in his view, been lost. It is likely also the case that this reformation served geopolitical ends, allowing him to consolidate his power by (1) reasserting the city of Jerusalem's importance relative to other cities within Judah (e.g., worship at cultic locations outside of Jerusalem was forbidden) and by (2) reasserting Judah's independence from the regional powers that had been putting pressure on Judah (e.g., by forbidding the worship of non-Israelite Gods within the Kingdom of Judah). That is to say, Josiah sought to reassert the unique religious and political identity of the Kingdom of Judah and to reinforce Jerusalem as the epicenter of Judah's power. However, if Jerusalem and its temple were to serve these roles, the temple needed to be cleansed and repaired. So, Josiah sent workmen to the temple to remove any images of other deities that had been introduced onto the temple grounds and to do any needed physical repairs. It is not explicitly stated, but the implication is that the temple was in a state of disrepair, spiritually and physically.

In the course of the temple repair efforts, Hilkiah the high priest "found the book of the law in the house of the LORD" (2 Kings 22:8).[1] Apparently, Hilkiah discovered a previously un-

---

1. It is a little unclear what this means. On the one hand, if taken literally, perhaps as part of cleaning out and cleaning up the temple the workers stumbled upon an unknown text that had been stashed away in a forgotten corner. However, from a literary perspective, this framing could also be a storytelling device to ascribe additional authoritative status to a specific text (i.e. it was a temple text). In either instance, there is a body of scholarship that suggests the text in question here is, more or less, what we now call Deuteronomy. However, as is the case with other Hebrew Bible books, Deuteronomy—in whatever form it was created/found—was edited and redacted over time, probably coming near completion during

known version of God's instruction. Hilkiah gave the book to the scribe Shaphan, who in turn took the book to King Josiah and read it to him. Upon hearing the words of the book, King Josiah "rent his clothes" (2 Kings 22:11). King Josiah's reaction suggests that, upon hearing the law as articulated in this new book, he was concerned with how far the Kingdom of Judah had strayed from God's instructions. King Josiah's instinct was to use this book of teachings as the basis for his reform efforts. However, before moving forward too rashly, King Josiah wanted to validate the veracity of this newly discovered instruction. So Josiah issued a command: "Go ye, inquire of the LORD for me, and for the people, and for all Judah, concerning the words of this book that is found: for great is the wrath of the LORD that is kindled against us, because our fathers have not hearkened unto the words of this book, to do according unto all that which is written concerning us" (2 Kings 22:14). And this is where it gets really interesting.

The Prophetess

Hilkiah and Shaphan (and a couple of others) had a decision to make. How would they accomplish the king's charge to validate that the book is from God? The king did not express

---

the time of the Babylonian exile. Thus, Deuteronomy as we have it now, captures the ancient memory of Sinai but also reflects the concerns of those who experienced invasion and exile centuries later. As a result, Deuteronomy both expounds the law (as we see in Exodus), but also includes a layer of exile-adjacent explanations, reasoning, and theologizing. This interpretive view, often called Deuteronomistic History, is thought to have originated in the Northern Kingdom as a response to the Assyrian invitation and to have been further developed in the Southern Kingdom in response to the Babylonian invasion. Because Deuteronomistic History is 'looking back' from the vantage point of invasion and exile, in some instances it provides explanations, reasons, or theologizing that differ from those provided in other Torah texts (e.g. Exodus 20:8–11 says that Sabbath remembers creation, whereas Deuteronomy 5:12–15 says Sabbath remembers the exodus from Egypt).

a preference on who, exactly, should be the one to validate the truth of this newly discovered book of scripture—he left that up to his envoys. So, who should Hilkiah and Shaphan (and the others) ask to inquire of the LORD—on behalf of the king, the people, and for all of Judah—whether or not this new book came from God? There are at least three options for accomplishing this task that would make sense from an LDS perspective.

❖ **HILKIAH** Hilkiah is identified as the High Priest, meaning he was likely a direct descendant of Aaron and among the most senior individuals, if not *the* most senior individual, in the priestly hierarchy at the temple. He had a birthright claim to the Aaronic Priesthood. In other words, Hilkiah had the authority to be responsible for the proper administration of God's proscribed ordinances (in common LDS parlance, he "presided" at the temple). By virtue of his position, he would have been the one to enter the Holy of Holies, the most sacred part of the temple, on *Yom Kippur*—quite an honor. And, given that Hilkiah was helping with King Josiah's reform efforts, including specifically rejuvenating the temple, it seems reasonable to believe that he was recognized as a man of God who possessed both priestly authority and leadership responsibilities and would thus be a reasonable candidate to answer the king's question.

❖ **JEREMIAH** According to the writings of Jeremiah, the prophet Jeremiah, who would later see Jerusalem and the temple destroyed and is credited with writing Lamentations, began his ministry in the 13th year of Josiah's rule (Jeremiah 1:2), when King Josiah was about 21 years old. This was five years before the beginning of the Josianic reforms.[2] Assuming this dating is correct, by the time of King Josiah's reform, Jeremiah was likely a well-established prophetic figure in Jerusalem (see also 1 Nephi 5:13, 7:14). He was a known prophet who spoke for God. What's more, the LDS community also asserts that prophets like Jeremiah, at some point that is unrecorded, received the Melchizedek Priesthood (even though the Hebrew Bible is strikingly silent on this claim, here and in every other instance). From an LDS perspective, this would further strengthen the view that Jeremiah could serve as an authoritative arbiter of God's will and be able to opine on the authenticity of this text.

ZEPHANIAH According to the writings of Zephaniah, the prophet Zephaniah was also operating during the reign of King Josiah (Zephaniah 1:1).[3] Zephaniah's writings suggest his primary audience was the people of Jerusalem. This means that both Jeremiah and Zephaniah were prophesying around the same time and place. Like Jeremiah, Zephaniah is serving as God's mouthpiece and speaking on God's behalf to the people—he is a recognized prophet. Again, the LDS community would also assert that, at some point that is unrecorded, Zephaniah received the Melchizedek Priesthood and thus held the proper authority to resolve a question about the veracity of the text found in the temple.

---

2. Interestingly, Jeremiah is not mentioned at all in 2 Kings.

3. Some scholars suggest that the writings of Zephaniah, in their current form came together much later, but were based on an earlier version (potentially which aligns with the timing that is internally suggested) which still forms the core of the message.

Any of these three men would seem like an obvious option when it comes to inquiring of the LORD about whether this new book of scripture was of divine origin. After all, this was no small matter; this new book would guide the reform efforts for the entire Kingdom of Judah. King Josiah, the people, and all of Judah needed to be *certain* that this new book of scripture came from God, so whoever was asked to intervene on their behalf would need to (1) have an unquestionable ability to speak *to* and *for* God, and (2) have the authority to provide a response that could be trusted by the king, the people, and all of Judah as the word of the LORD.

So, who did the envoys of the king ask to take on this deeply significant and weighty task? Well, instead of asking any of the men described above, the envoys of the king sought out *the Prophetess Huldah*.

As stated at the beginning of the chapter, we know very little about Huldah. In the KJV it says, "she dwelt in Jerusalem in the college;" in the NRSV it says, she was "the keeper of the wardrobe; she resided in Jerusalem in the Second Quarter;" and in the JPS it says she was "the keeper of the wardrobe— who was living in Jerusalem in the Mishneh." So we know she lived in a specific part of Jerusalem and that perhaps, as a profession, she kept track of priestly apparel or the king's apparel when it was not in use—the details are sparse. But we do know this without question: *she was a prophetess*. And she was respected enough that when the stakes were exceptionally high, when the people absolutely needed a direct link to the LORD, the temple's high priest took the question to her instead of anyone else. And her answer, which you can read in 2 Kings 22:15–20 or 2 Chronicles 34:23–27, was authoritative enough that it was accepted without question by King Josiah, the people, and all of Judah. That is right: just her word alone—just the word of the prophetess—was authoritative and powerful enough for Josiah to begin reforming the entire kingdom based on this new text. Not too shabby for a woman.

How do we explain this in an LDS Church where being male is a prerequisite for being a prophet? There are other women explicitly identified as prophetesses in the Hebrew Bible: Miriam (Exodus 15:20), Deborah (Judges 4:4), and Noadiah (Nehemiah 6:14), and Isaiah's wife (Isaiah 8:3),[4] but, in the LDS Church, women cannot bear this title, hold this authority, or have this responsibility. I suppose we could twist ourselves into intellectual knots trying to explain how these scriptures do not mean what they seem on their face to mean—"they're not really prophetesses, this is probably just one more example of the Bible being translated incorrectly." Or we could try to explain away the existence of a female prophet—"inspiration is available to everyone but that does not necessarily mean she was a prophetess in the strict sense of the word." Or we dodge the issue altogether by asserting that such things are a relic of the past—"only ancient Israel needed this and the modern church does not."

Or, we could take the text at face value. We could just accept that Huldah was a prophetess. We could just accept that the king, high priest, and all the people believed and trusted that she had the power and authority to speak for God. We could just accept that Huldah was, in fact, God's chosen mouthpiece to the people. We could just accept that a woman *was indeed* a prophet.

---

4. Some have suggested that in the case of Isaiah's wife, who is unnamed, what is meant is "the prophet's wife." But the underlying Hebrew is in Isaiah so similar to the Hebrew in the other instances referenced—they all use han·nə·ḇî·'āh: "the" (han) "prophet (nə·ḇî) "ess" ('āh)—that I find this suggestion unconvincing. In addition to the women mentioned above, Jonathan Stapley notes the existence of secondhand accounts of Joseph and Hyrum Smith asserting that the woman of En-dor (1 Sam 28) "was actually Samuel's wife, a woman of God, and a prophetess." See Jonathan A. Stapley. *The Power of Godliness, Mormon Liturgy and the Cosmos.* pg. 105.

And if we do that—that is to say, if we take the Hebrew Bible seriously—then we need to carefully consider the implications of what that might mean for our modern church and the roles that women have within it. And I feel like that's a conversation worth having.

CHAPTER 14

Psalms as a Model for Wholeness[1]

As psychiatrist Curt Thompson puts it, emotions are "not opinions to be countered," rather they are "true experiences that require attention."[2] This is because human experience is emotional experience, and emotional experience is human experience. Emotions are one of the critical ways that our brain organizes, understands, and anticipates the world around us. In fact, sociologist Eduardo Bericat takes this idea further, asserting that human beings "can only experience life emotionally."[3] Emotions are neither good nor bad; they are simply information we process, just like touch and taste.

That emotional experience is central to our life on earth is affirmed in official LDS Church sources. The Church's Emotional Resilience manual notes that "emotions are a normal part of our mortal experience."[4] Expanding on this idea, in a digital

---

1. Portions of this chapter, now modified, appeared in *Public Square Magazine* on August 15, 2022 under the title "Trusting God to See our Whole Heart," https://publicsquaremag.org/faith/gospel-fare/trusting-god-to-see-our-whole-heart/

2. Curt Thompson. *Anatomy of the Soul,* p. 96.

3. As quoted in Brene Brown. *Atlas of the Heart,* p. xxiii.

4. *Finding Strength in the Lord: Emotional Resilience.* The Church of Jesus Christ of Latter-day Saints, p. 49. https://www.churchofjesuschrist.

supplement to the April 2019 *Ensign* magazine, psychologist Dr. Debra Theobald McClendon notes, "feelings, both positive and negative, serve a functional purpose and can bless your life as you learn from the information they provide."[5] And in language that is a little less formal, Elder Jeffrey R. Holland observes, "We all have highs and lows. . . . Beautiful sunshine brings encouragement. A good night's sleep usually works wonders. But there are times in all of our lives when deep sorrow or suffering or fear or loneliness makes us cry out for the peace which only God . . . can bring."[6] Said directly, emotions just *are*.

But even if we set aside professional and pastoral views on emotion, as a matter of doctrine, we in the LDS Church believe in a God whose eternal life includes and incorporates the full spectrum of emotions—the theological language here is that we believe in a God that is *passible*: "capable of feeling or suffering."[7] Perhaps the most thorough discussion of the LDS Church's views on divine passibility can be found in Terryl and Fiona Givens' book *The God Who Weeps*.[8] Briefly, LDS doctrine believes in a God who weeps, laughs, cries, and exults. President Russell M. Nelson sums up this reality with characteristic simplicity and directness: "God is not devoid of emotions."[9] God feels.

org/study/manual/emotional-resilience-for-self-reliance/3-our-bodies-and-emotions

5. Debra Theobald McClendon. "Discerning Your Feelings: Anxiety or the Spirit?" *Ensign.* https://www.churchofjesuschrist.org/study/ensign/2019/04/young-adults/discerning-your-feelings-anxiety-or-the-spirit

6. Jeffrey R. Holland, "The Peaceable Things of the Kingdom" October 1996 General Conference.

7. *Merriam-Webster.com Dictionary*, "passible," accessed May 28, 2023, https://www.merriam-webster.com/dictionary/passible.

8. Terryl and Fiona Givens, *The God Who Weeps, How Mormons Make Sense of Life.*

9. President Russell M. Nelson, *Facebook*, Dec. 24, 2021, available at: https://www.facebook.com/russell.m.nelson.

The implications of this doctrinal position are profound when it comes to understanding the role that emotions play in our own lives here on Earth and in our eternal lives in the world to come. Because we believe in a God that is passible, it means that, for each of us, coming to know (John 17:3) and becoming like God (1 John 3:2) means embracing the full spectrum of emotional experiences that we encounter in this life. That is to say, emotions are not something to be overcome, nor should we expect that eventually all of the "bad" emotions will go away and only the "good" emotions will remain. Rather, eternal life includes the integration of our emotional experiences as part of the process of eternal progression. If God can both weep and rejoice because God can feel both sadness and joyfulness, then why should we expect anything different? The reality is that *eternal exaltation is not a process of shedding our emotions; rather, exaltation includes the eternalization of our emotional experiences.*

However, in modern Christian there is a tendency to assign moral value to specific emotions—particularly when it comes to acts of religious practice. Feelings of gratitude, praise, peace, happiness, thanksgiving, and contentedness (for instance) are associated with righteousness and seen as appropriate vehicles for worship, whereas feelings of anxiousness, tenseness, anger, sadness, and despair (for example) are associated with unrighteousness and seen as inappropriate vehicles for worship.[10] The functional result of this approach to emotion is a crippling of our progression: if only a part of our emotional experience is seen as 'fit' for our religious practice then we can only bring a part of ourselves to our worship. We cannot be whole because social conventions dictate that only some emotions are suitable for engagement with God. Said another way,

---

10. Kate Bowler does as good a job as anyone in exploring the implications of a praise-focused Christian worldview. See, for instance, *Everything Happens for a Reason and Other Lies I've Loved.*

when certain aspects of our emotional lives are seen as inappropriate for our religious practice, we limit our ability to engage in a full and truly open relationship with God and with each other. In my view, trading away wholeness to accommodate social expectations damages us individually and collectively.

Thank the heavens that we have the Psalms!

The Book of Psalms (or the Psalter) explores worship from all its different emotional angles. Rather than God-talk that is only self-assuredly praise-centric, the Psalter opens the door for worship language that encompasses the entirety of the human experience. So yes, at times the Psalmist is a voice of praise, but at other times the Psalmist's voice is one of lament; at times the psalmist sings songs of thanksgiving, and at other times the Psalmist expresses disorientation; at times the psalmist embraces God's dominion over everything, and at other times the Psalmist wonders why God feels absent. This kind of multivocality, when it comes to God-talk, is (unfortunately) foreign to modern ears. In fact, the challenge this kind of language presents has led some to simply 'skip over' the more difficult psalms (after all, what is one to do with Psalm 137? . . . go read it . . . including the last verse). But in skipping over the more difficult psalms, we inadvertently close ourselves off to the reality that *all* emotional states can be places of worship and that every experience, even (and maybe especially) the hard ones, can serve as a starting point for a dialogue with God.

So how does this play out in the Psalter? Consider the different approaches taken in Psalm 111 (a psalm expressing praise) and Psalm 13 (a psalm expressing lament). In Psalm 111 we encounter a psalmist brimming with feelings of peace and contentment. "Praise ye the LORD," the Psalmist shouts, "I will praise the LORD with *my* whole heart. . . . The works of the LORD *are* great." It is not hard to imagine such language coming at the birth of a long-awaited child or the conclusion of a sore trial. This psalm shows us that the language of praise can be a language of worship. Now consider Psalm 13, where we encounter a poet near the end of her rope who is burdened by anxiety and pain. "How long wilt thou forget me, O LORD? for ever? How long wilt thou hide thy face from me?" the Psalmist laments, "How long shall I take counsel in my soul, having sorrow in my heart daily?" It is not hard to imagine such language coming at the death of a loved one, or from the deepest recesses of an overwhelming trial. But remarkably, the psalms teach us that lament is also a language of worship. The language of lament gives a way to speak to God authentically when the world is crumbling all around. The psalms show us that praise and lament are simply different sides of the human experience and that both can be holy when brought to God.

Again, consider two more psalms: Psalm 100 (a psalm expressing thanksgiving) and Psalm 74 (a psalm expressing disorientation). In Psalm 100, we encounter a poet for whom all the pieces have finally fallen into place. "Make a joyful noise unto the LORD," the Psalmist shouts, "we are his people, and the sheep of his pasture . . . be thankful unto him, and bless his name." It is not hard to imagine such language coming at the arrival of good fortune (earned or by chance) or the view of a mountain vista. This psalm shows us that thanksgiving is a language of worship. Now consider Psalm 74, where we encounter a psalmist who is struggling to make sense of life's vagaries. "Why doth thine anger smoke against the sheep of thy pasture?" the Psalmist wonders, "have respect unto the covenant: for the dark places of the earth are full of the habitations of cruelty." It is not hard to imagine such language coming from one who, despite earnest efforts and righteous striving, has suffered misfortune after misfortune and whose world feels chaotic and unsettled.[11] This psalm teaches us that disorientation is also a language of worship. In the midst of

---

11. This psalm was likely written in response to the destruction of Jerusalem and the razing of the temple by the Babylonians. Seen in that light, it

the tempest, feelings of confusion and struggle voiced to God are feelings given to God and thus become the most sacred of offerings. These psalms show us that thanksgiving and disorientation are simply different sides of the human experience and that both can be holy when brought to God.

The point here, and I think a key lesson we can take from the Psalter collectively, is that a real relationship with God must be wholly authentic and wholly complete. Nothing can be held back. For that to be true, the full spectrum of emotional experience should be included in our worship. *All emotional experiences can be offered to God.* All emotional experiences become opportunities for a deepened relationship with the Divine.[12] All emotional experiences can be holy. And this is exactly why the Psalms are such a critical component of our continued engagement with the Hebrew Bible. The Psalms provide a thundering and resounding rejection of any theology, ideology, or philosophy that privileges a praise-only approach to worship, or that categorizes feelings like anxiousness, tenseness, anger, sadness, and despair as feelings that must be "overcome" *before* "real worship" can happen. The Psalms sacralize all aspects of the human experience. Thus, we see in the Psalms that no emotional experience is left on the cutting room floor.

In his exploration of another of the more challenging psalms (Psalm 109), scholar Walter Brueggemann observed that the speech of the Psalms " is precious because it shows that Israel understood that what is *healthily human* intersects

---

is not hard to understand the sense of disorientation that permeates this particular psalm.

12. To be exceptionally clear, I hold out the hope that mental illness (like any illness) can be a catalyst for a deeper encounter with the divine. That does not mean, however, that individuals who are sick—with any ailment—should forgo seeking the support of licensed, trained professionals when appropriate. Seeking help does not prevent the sacralization of our experience.

with what is *vitally faithful*."[13] As we embrace the full spectrum of our emotional experience and bring all of it more fully into our worship, we create the foundation for deepened, authentic relationships with those around us and with God. Curt Thompson frames it thusly: emotion "is one of the most important means by which [we] comprehend [our] experiences in life,"[14] and thus, I might add, it is also one of the most important means by which we comprehend our experiences with God.

God does not expect us to shed our human experience (as if it were a skin to be shed) by demanding that we excise the challenging emotional experiences of life from our spiritual journeys. Rather, the miracle of God's work is that it transforms our very humanity into something divine. This happens not by cutting off parts and pieces of what makes us human, but by incorporating the entire human experience—including the full spectrum of our emotional experience—into a grand tapestry of restoration and renewal. This is the message of the Psalms.

---

13. Walter Brueggemann. *The Message of the Psalms*, p. 86. Emphasis original.

14. Curt Thompson. *Anatomy of the Soul*, p. 105.

CHAPTER 15

On Reading Isaiah[1]

It is hard in the 21st Century—with more than 1 billion Christians and with two millennia of Christian apologetics and tradition behind us—to appreciate the challenge that Jesus presented to his Jewish adherents in the first century. According to the Gospels, here was a practicing Jew who understood and could explain the Torah and the teaching of the prophets with striking clarity and profound insight, and yet the authority by which he claimed to teach seemed (to some) to put him at odds with the same sacred text from which he taught.[2] Here was a person whose insights were deeply rooted in the Torah and the prophetic literature but who also, simultaneously, understood this tradition in ways that many found uncomfortable and others found problematic. Here was a Jew who was not a local politician, and yet who taught things and acted in ways that challenged, at the most fundamental levels, the social equilibrium of his day. Though it may be hard for Christians of the 21st Century to see it sometimes, Jesus was a po-

---

1. Portions of this chapter, now modified, appeared in *Public Square Magazine* on September 20, 2022. See https://publicsquaremag.org/faith/gospel-fare/seeing-old-and-new-things-in-isaiah/
2. The different New Testament Gospels portray how and by whom this claim of authority was made.

lemical figure who drew out intense reactions—positive and negative—from those with whom he interacted.

Thus, it is not surprising that Jesus's detractors and followers both scrambled to find sacred texts to support their respective positions regarding Jesus—each group looking for a way to "explain away" or "explain" Jesus. There are numerous examples in the Gospels of Jesus's detractors challenging his teachings and actions based on Hebrew Bible texts. They brought core Jewish teachings to Jesus (e.g., teachings on the Sabbath Day) and, in essence, asked him "how can you do/teach [this thing] when our sacred text seems to say something contrary?" That this happened should not be at all surprising. Throughout religious history, including in modern Christianity, when there is a sense that someone is teaching/doing something that is seen as contrary to established practice or doctrine, individuals dig back into their sacred tradition to ground their disapproval in authoritative texts.

Conversely, Jesus's followers did the same thing after his death—they mined sacred text to marshal support for the cause of Jesus. A prime example of this is the presence of the fulfillment citations in the Gospel of Matthew.[3] That Gospel writer used the language ". . . that it might be fulfilled . . ." to expressly link the prophetic language of Isaiah, Jeremiah, and Hosea (among others) with Jesus's actions and teachings. Matthew's Gospel saw in Israel's sacred texts a theological trajectory that could encompass Jesus and his mission. In fact, to one degree or another, nearly all of the New Testament texts seek to ground the authoritative nature of Jesus's coming, mission, death, and/or resurrection somewhere in the Hebrew Bible. Though the New Testament's way of re-reading the Hebrew Bible may feel like a self-evident approach for modern Christians 2, 000 years later, in its day, this was a dramatic act of re-see-

---

3. See Matthew 1:22-23; 2:15, 17–18, 23; 4:14–16; 8:17; 12:17–21; 13:35; 21:4–5; and 27:9–10.

ing ancient scripture with new eyes and within the new light of Jesus's advent. These early Christians, most of whom were Jewish Christians, re-heard the ancient prophetic language of their own faith tradition and, in so doing, found texts that they believed supported the doctrine Jesus taught and that seemed to be open to Jesus's divine, messianic mission. It was a truly and remarkably innovative interpretative exercise.

So why does this matter? In the LDS Church, we place a lot of stock in the writings of Isaiah—the most quoted Hebrew Bible prophet in the LDS standard works.[4] And, in a way that is not markedly different from many other Christian denominations' readings of this profound piece of literature, the LDS community is encouraged to see references to, and prophecies of, Jesus in the writings of Isaiah. To be clear, "finding Jesus" in the book of Isaiah (or other Hebrew Bible texts) is a defensible interpretive move. However, nearly 2, 000 years removed from the early Christians' first attempts to "find" Jesus in the texts that would become the Hebrew Bible, it is sometimes too easy for the LDS community, and for all Christians generally, to forget how novel this understanding of the Hebrew Bible was in the first centuries of Christianity: this was a bold and daring reinterpretation of the core texts that had grounded the faith tradition of Israel. But in our time, we have become so accustomed to seeing the Hebrew Bible through a Christian lens that it is easy (too easy) to slip into the belief that the Christian view is the only legitimate reading . . . to the exclusion of all other understandings. And that is problematic.

The most recent *Come, Follow Me* materials to cover Isaiah note plainly that "for the most part, people today are not

---

4. See "Why Is Isaiah the Most Quoted Prophet in the Bible?" for a contemporary, non-LDS view, of the use of Isaiah in the New Testament: https://www.christianity.com/wiki/bible/why-is-isaiah-the-most-quoted-prophet-in-the-bible.html. See Fair Latter-day Saints for a discussion of Isaiah texts in the Mormon: https://www.fairlatterdaysaints.org/answers/Isaiah_and_the_Book_of_Mormon.

the primary audience of the Old Testament prophets. Those prophets had immediate concerns they were addressing in their time and place—just as our Latter-day prophets address our immediate concerns today." The *Come, Follow Me* materials also note that, "prophets can also look beyond immediate concerns . . . they teach eternal truths, relevant to any age."[5] In other words, there are multiple ways to understand the same text. As a case in point, the *Come, Follow Me* materials point to Isaiah 40:3: "The voice of him that crieth in the wilderness, Prepare ye the way of the Lord." These Church-produced materials note that this verse can be read at least three ways: (1) as a message to captive Jews in Babylon that God would free them (probably how it was originally understood); (2) as a reference to John the Baptist, as we see happen in the Gospels of Matthew, Mark, and Luke (a re-seeing of this verse in the new light of Jesus's advent); and (3) as a prophecy still being fulfilled today in preparation for Christ's second coming (when considered within the context of the 'continuing Restoration').

The notion that the same verse can be read in multiple ways is true for scriptures like Isaiah 7:14–16, Isaiah 9:6–7; Isaiah 11:1–12, and Isaiah 53:2–12. Yes, Christians can see in these specific verses of scripture opaque allusions to Jesus in their references to Immanuel, "God with Us" (Isaiah 7); the prince of peace (Isaiah 9); the one with wisdom and understanding (Isaiah 11); and he who was wounded for our transgression (Isaiah 53). This is the approach the early Christians took. But—and I want to be clear about this—it is *not* the only interpretive approach and (as is noted with the *Come, Follow Me* discussion of prophetic texts quoted above), it is true that

---

5. The Church of Jesus Christ of Latter-day Saints, "Prophets and Prophecy" *Come, Follow Me*, available at https://www.churchofjesuschrist.org/study/manual/come-follow-me-for-individuals-and-families-old-testament-2022/37-thoughts

"[Isaiah] had immediate concerns that [he] was addressing in [his] time and place."

In their own time, the texts that would eventually form the writings of Isaiah, had profound meaning for those who heard them. (And they continue to have profound meaning for the Jewish community, which also draws strength from these same texts without superimposing a Christian gloss!) Consistent with the theological approach of Isaiah, in their own day these texts likely pointed to the hope that God would establish (Isaiah 7) a theopolitical leader (Isaiah 9) through the Davidic line that would be more attentive to the Torah's requirements, specifically those related to communal care, resulting in a kingdom of peace and prosperity for a reunited Israel (Isaiah 11), and that Israel's struggle to establish this kingdom would be redemptive for all the people of the world (Isaiah 53). This reading—one that may feel foreign to some in the LDS community—provides valuable and different insights into God's interactions with humankind.

It is important to honor the Christian understanding of the Hebrew Bible. But it is equally important to honor non-Christian understandings of the Hebrew Bible. And I believe that honoring both, simultaneously, *increases* our appreciation for these sacred texts. Speaking of Isaiah, scholar Walter Brueggemann notes:

> The book of Isaiah has been a fertile interpretive field for Christian theology . . . but it must always be recognized that much Christian reading has flatly preempted the text and forced upon the text readings that are far removed from its seemingly clear intent. . . . It's legitimate to see how the book of Isaiah fed, nurtured, and evoked Christian imagination with reference to Jesus. But that is very different from any claim that the book of Isaiah predicts or specifically anticipates Jesus. Such a preemption, as has often occurred in reading of the church, constitutes not only a failure

> to respect Jewish readers, but is a distortion of
> the book itself. It is strongly preferable, I suggest,
> that Jews and Christians together recognize that
> the book of Isaiah is enormously and generatively
> open in more than one tradition.[6]

In short, and said slightly differently, when we fail to honor both readings, side-by-side, we do ourselves, the book of Isaiah, and the prophetic tradition a disservice.

As just one example of how reading the scripture through a non-Christian lens might offer value in our modern LDS Church, consider Isaiah 9:6–7: "For unto us a child is born, unto us a son is given: and the government shall be upon his shoulder: and his name shall be called Wonderful, Counsellor, The mighty God, The everlasting Father, The Prince of Peace. Of the increase of his government and peace there shall be no end, upon the throne of David, and upon his kingdom, to order it, and to establish it with judgment and with justice from henceforth even for ever. The zeal of the Lord of hosts will perform this." In part due to Handel's Messiah, there is likely a large swath of Christianity that cannot see these verses as anything other than a prophecy of Jesus. So, what else could these verses mean?

In his own time and place and facing significant geopolitical pressures (it is unclear whether that pressure is from the Assyrians in the north or Syro-Ephraimite pressure in the south),[7] Isaiah offers the royal court the prophetic promise of an heir to David's throne who will free Israel from the anxieties caused by external threats to sovereignty. This king— whose name describes the saving acts of God on behalf of God's people (not the character of the person himself; in the same vein as other Hebrew Bible names: e.g., Isaiah = "The

---

6. Walter Brueggemann. *Isaiah, Vol. 1: Chapters 1–39*, pp.5–6

7. Adele Berlin and Marc Zvi Brettler, eds, *The Jewish Study Bible*, 2nd ed. pg. 784 fn to Isaiah 9:1–6.

LORD Saves," Joshua = "The LORD is Salvation," Hezekiah = "The LORD Strengthens")—will establish a kingdom based on justice (*mishpat*) and righteousness (*tsedeq*).

As Isaiah makes clear in other places (see Isaiah 1:10–17), and as is discussed in greater detail in the next chapter of this book, the LORD wants a people who prioritize the protection of those who are vulnerable to exploitation and who actively care for those who need it. In Isaiah 9:6–7, Isaiah suggests that it is a kingdom built on these principles that will be able to finally provide the peace that the people so desperately seek. In language more comfortable to modern LDS readers: Isaiah is telling the people that, if they want real, lasting peace and freedom from outside forces, rather than focusing on military strength or diplomacy, they need to look inward and establish a Zion community—a community where care for "the other" is the overarching concern of its citizenry and the primary cause of those in power. Isaiah suggests that this is the kind of kingdom that will stand "for ever."

Isaiah says that real freedom and lasting peace are, in the end, not founded on geopolitical stratagem or national might, but instead found in a society where the Torah's requirements of care and concern for everyone, including for those who are not part of the community (the "strangers"), guide the actions of all. This is because, according to Isaiah, such freedom and peace cannot come from human action. Rather, the "zeal of the Lord of hosts will perform this." It is God—who is Wonderful, Counsellor, The mighty God, The everlasting Father, The Prince of Peace—that liberates; and the God that liberates requires a people who live by the principles of justice and righteousness.

That reading, entirely outside of a Christian lens, is—in my view—just as powerful as any Christianized reading and just as relevant to our modern time as it was in the 8th century BCE. In a world of geopolitical pressures, is lasting peace and security to be found in the principles of justice and righteousness? Isaiah says it is. In a world where violence and the threat of violence surrounds us nearly all the time (at the individual, community, and nation-state levels), do we really believe in the "zeal of the Lord of hosts" to establish peace? Isaiah says we should. And, perhaps most importantly, are we willing (at the individual, community, and nation-state levels) to prioritize covenant-care for those around us, including the "strangers"? Isaiah says that is the only way to find the peace we seek.

CHAPTER 16

Unpacking Isaiah 58 and the Charge of Communal Care

"To what purpose is the multitude of your sacrifices unto me? Saith the LORD."

This question, posed in the opening chapter of the book of Isaiah, put Israel in an uncomfortable position.[1]

That specific sacrifices, rituals, feasts, and other religious practices were centrally related to Israel's covenant with God was beyond doubt. Israel's sacred texts clearly outlined how and in what way Israel was to worship the God of the Exodus and Sinai (see, for instance, Exodus 12:14; 13:13; 20:22–23:33; Exodus 34:11–26; Deuteronomy 12–26; Leviticus 17–26 as a start). And, apparently, Israel generally did the things it had been asked to do. Israel observed the Sabbath, practiced temple rituals (including sacrifices), and held the appropriate festivals.

And yet, multiple prophets challenged Israel's adherence to the very practices that were part of this prophetically given guide to worship. Prophet after prophet chastised Israel even

---

1. Portions of this chapter, now modified, appeared in *Public Square Magazine* on December 9, 2022. Available at: https://publicsquaremag.org/faith/gospel-fare/why-did-god-punich-ancient-israel/

as Israel followed the requirements it was given regarding sacrifices, rituals, and feasts and rituals. Picking up where the question above leaves off, Isaiah continues voicing God's view of these practices:

> I [the LORD] am full of the burnt offerings of rams, and the fat of fed beasts; and I delight not in the blood of bullocks, or of lambs, or of he goats. . . . Bring no more vain oblations; incense is an abomination unto me; the new moons and sabbaths, the calling of assemblies, I cannot away with; it is iniquity, even the solemn meeting. Your new moons and your appointed feasts my soul hateth: they are a trouble unto me; I am weary to bear them. And when ye spread forth your hands, I will hide mine eyes from you: yea, when ye make many prayers, I will not hear: your hands are full of blood. (Isaiah 1:11–15).

To be clear, the LORD does more than *just* summarily dismiss Israel's ongoing worship practices; the LORD says that these religious rites—the sacrifices, rituals, and feasts they are under obligation to keep—are "iniquity," and an "abomination, and that "my soul hateth" them! This scathing condemnation concludes by the LORD saying, "I will hide mine eyes from you . . . I will not hear you."

And Isaiah was not alone in portraying God's displeasure with Israel's worship. We see similar language in the book of Amos. Amos frames it this way:

> I [the LORD] hate, I despise your feast days, and I will not smell in your solemn assemblies. Though ye offer me burnt offerings and your meat offerings, I will not accept them: neither will I regard the peace offerings of your fat beasts. Take thou away from me the noise of thy songs; for I will not hear the melody of thy viols. (Amos 5:21–23)

And Hosea says simply:

> They sacrifice flesh for the sacrifices of mine offer-
> ings, and eat it; but the LORD accepteth them not.
> (Hosea 8:13)

Just as we see in Isaiah's language, the language of Amos and Hosea portray the LORD as more than just critiquing the act of worship. Isaiah, Amos, and Hosea collectively say that the LORD despises Israel's feasts, refuses to accept (or even regard!) its offerings and sacrifices, and calls Israel's songs and music of praise "noise" that "I will not hear."

The prophet Micah takes a different approach but delivers the same basic message as his prophetic contemporaries. After articulating all the things that the LORD has done for Israel from Egypt onward, Micah asks Israel a series of stinging rhetorical questions that serve to undermine Israel's acts of worship:

> Wherewith shall I come before the Lord, and bow
> myself before the high God? . . . Will the Lord be
> pleased with thousands of rams, or with ten thou-
> sands of rivers of oil? shall I give my firstborn for
> my transgression, the fruit of my body for the sin
> of my soul? (Micah 6:6–7)

The clear answer to Micah's hyperbolic questions about whether God is pleased by the prospect of "thousands of rams" or "ten thousands of rivers of oil" or even "my first born" is *no*. Over-the-top zeal is not only insufficient, but is, itself, a source of God's disapproval. Isaiah, Amos, Hosea, and Micah all make clear that, despite Israel's apparent exact obedience to required sacrifices, rituals, feasts, and other religious practices, God is displeased with Israel.

So, what is Israel doing wrong? At least one answer is easily pushed aside. I have heard some suggest that there is something wrong (or lacking) in the teachings that God gave at Sinai. The LORD is displeased with Israel's adherence to the requirements of the Mosaic Law because the Mosaic Law is *itself* displeasing or incomplete. However, a later prophet, Ezekiel, makes it clear that this *cannot* be the case. In Ezekiel's vision of restoration, the temple that is to be rebuilt in Jerusalem as part of this restoration of Israel is marked by close ritual observance to the very same requirements that are outlined in Exodus, Deuteronomy, and Leviticus (See Ezekiel 42), and that were apparently being followed at the time when Isaiah, Amos, Hosea, and Micah voiced God's frustration with Israel. Similarly, the first six chapters of the Book of Ezra—which chronicle Israel's return from exile to the promised land—are focused on reestablishing these same sacrifices, rituals, feasts, and other religious practices that served as markers of Israel's faithfulness to God. If the law was the problem, Israel's prophetic visions of restoration and acts of reestablishment would have corrected it—but rather than changing these requirements, they doubled-down on them. Thus, the problem Isaiah, Amos, Hosea, and Micah point to is not with patterns of worship.

Another explanation for Isaiah, Amos, Hosea, and Micah's critique that can be similarly brushed aside is the notion that Israel was knowingly "going through the motions"—they were guilty of willful hypocrisy. That is to say, that in offering sacrifices or participating in festivals, Israel was not actually worshiping God, and knew it was not worshiping God. Instead, Israel was intentionally fulfilling outward requirements without any attempt at deeper covenantal connection, because somehow Israel believed that outward performance was enough. Yet, this does not seem to be the primary source of the problem either. It was certainly the case that Israel did not always love and worship the LORD and keep the Sinai teaching in their respective hearts as was supposed to happen (See Deuteronomy 6:5–6).[2] In fact, highlighting Israel's penchant for

---

2. When the act of worship becomes more important than the purpose of worship, what I labeled 'ecclesiolatry' in an earlier chapter, one strays into potential idol worship.

straying and losing focus, a central hope in Ezekiel's prophetic language is that Israel will be given a "new heart" (see Ezekiel 36). However, while all of this might be true, hypocrisy does not seem to be the core problem. Only in Amos (and only in one verse, Amos 8:5) is there any indication that Israel was not focused on worshiping God. Indeed, it seems more likely that the people believed that they were doing things correctly. The people felt like they were worshiping God as they performed the required performances and rituals and kept the required observances. That is to say: I think Israel understood itself as keeping the commandments and, thus, being true to the covenant. In fact, I think a key indication that Israel felt like its adherence to sacrifices, rituals, feasts, and other religious practices was in line with God's expectations is the very fact that Isaiah, Amos, Hosea, and Micah had to use such dramatic language to get Israel's attention. Israel was falling short, and it needed to change, and may not have recognized this reality without a prophetic nudge (or sledgehammer as the case may be!) because it really believed things were just fine.

Justice, Righteousness, and Mercy: The Basis of Communal Care

So, what is it that Israel needed to do differently? Fortunately, in the same way that Isaiah, Amos, Hosea, and Micah were direct with Israel when it came to expressing the LORD's displeasure, these four prophets were similarly direct when it came to stating what Israel needed to do differently. And what was that? Put briefly: Israel needed to exercise justice, righteousness, and mercy. Here is how each of the four prophets express this:

> Learn to do well; seek judgment, relieve the oppressed, judge the fatherless, plead for the widow. . . . Zion shall be redeemed with judgment, and her converts with righteousness. (Isaiah 1:17, 27)

> But let judgment run down as waters, and righteousness as a mighty stream. (Amos 5:24)

> For I desired mercy, and not sacrifice; and the knowledge of God more than burnt offerings. (Hosea 6:6)

> He hath shewed thee, O man, what is good; and what doth the Lord require of thee, but to do justly, and to love mercy, and to walk humbly with thy God? (Micah 6:8)

My sense, especially in light of the earlier reference to Ezekiel and Ezra's view of the importance of Israel's ritual practices, is that God was not rejecting outright the method of worship that God had given Israel, nor was God impugning the motivation behind Israel's keeping of the required sacrifices, rituals, feasts, and other religious practices. Rather, Isaiah, Amos, Hosea, and Micah suggest that Israel needed to do a better job practicing what Jesus would call (eight centuries later) the "weightier matters" of the Sinaitic teachings (Matthew 23:23). Israel's core problem—according to Isaiah, Amos, Hosea, and Micah—was the lack of justice (*mishpat*), righteousness (*tsedeq*), and mercy (*hesed*).

It is worth pausing momentarily to discuss these ideas in greater detail.

JUSTICE   If said with just the right inflection, the word "justice" in our modern vernacular feels punitive. It is what happens to people when they do something wrong; "justice is served" could be a superhero's catchphrase when she nabs the bad guy. In the modern LDS community, that notion is broadened a little, and "justice" is something closer to a synonym for "fair" or "equitable." For example, the phrase "God is just" for many in the LDS community means something like "God gives you what you deserve, good or bad." However, both of these senses of the words are worlds away from what the 8th century BCE prophets meant when they used that word.

The word we translate as "justice" (or "judgement" or "just-ly") comes from the Hebrew word *mishpat*. *Mishpat* reflects the idea of ensuring that the weakest members of society are protected from exploitation. Usually, the term is used in connection with groups like widows, orphans, resident aliens, or the poor, and often in contexts where there are clear power differentials. For instance, during some sorts of civil dispute, a person who exercises *mishpat* will take the side of widows or orphans and defend them against those who are more powerful. In the Hebrew Bible, "justice" most often points to a social obligation to protect the weak and powerless from exploitation.

RIGHTEOUSNESS In modern-day usage, "righteousness" is often associated with personal piety. In the modern LDS Church, righteousness is seen as an inward characteristic that is reflected in outward commitment: the more closely one follows Church teachings, the more righteous one is, and vice versa. Thus, "righteous" is often used to describe those who believe and practice in ways that are fully consistent with church teachings (they demonstrate orthodoxy and orthopraxy). In the LDS community, righteousness—this blend of orthodoxy and orthopraxy—is manifest in many ways, for instance by maintaining a current temple recommend, or by studying the scriptures and praying regularly, or by accepting and fulfilling callings, or by "following the prophet." However, these four prophets meant something else when they used the word "righteous."

In the Hebrew Bible, *tsedeq* is the Hebrew word usually translated into the English word "righteousness" (and its derivatives). Like *mishpat*, *tsedeq* connotes a social obligation. As used by these prophets, *tsedeq* is characterized by the idea of proactively caring for those who are disadvantaged or pursuing communal flourishing even when it comes at the expense of self-interest. *Tsedeq* is often the companion virtue to *mishpat*. Where justice is protecting the weakest members of society from exploitation (defending them), righteousness is actively taking steps to help those who need it (uplifting them). As one example, if an Israelite had to sell his family's land inheritance to settle a debt, someone who exercises *tsedq* would take steps to redeem that debt and return the land to the family. As used by these four prophets, "righteousness" points to ensuring that those who are on the margins of society are proactively given what they need to prosper and flourish.

MERCY The word "mercy" is commonly used nowadays to capture the idea of being favored, and often undeservedly so. "Mercy" is used to describe the act of helping those whose behavior might not otherwise justify such magnanimity (or to describe receiving such help). In the LDS community, "mercy" is often presented as the opposite of "justice." If justice is getting what you deserve, then mercy is getting what you do not deserve. However, just like the words *mishpat* and *tsedeq*, this modern-day usage is not necessarily what the word "mercy" means in the Hebrew Bible.

The Hebrew word translated into English as "mercy" in the verses above is *hesed*.[3] In addition to "mercy" *hesed* is also translated in the King James Version variously as "kindness", "goodness," "favor," and "lovingkindness." Unfortunately, these translations really do not fully reflect the power of the word *hesed*. *Hesed* expresses the notion of deep love characterized by loyalty and fidelity that pours out of one and toward the other. In fact, the term *hesed* is often used to express how God feels about Israel (for example, *hesed* is used throughout the Psalms to describe God's feelings of affection for and commitment to Israel). *Hesed* is a commitment so deep it can always be trusted—it is the type of lovingkindness that is

---

3. A word that President Russell Nelson highlighted in his 2002 Liahona article, "The Everlasting Covenant," *Liahona,* October 2022. https://www.churchofjesuschrist.org/study/liahona/2022/10/04-the-everlasting-covenant

foundational to covenant relationships. Israelites who demonstrate *hesed* act with lovingkindness toward those around them because they feel a commitment and affection so deep that nothing could sway them from doing what is best for the object of their affections. *Hesed* is more than just a feeling; it pours out in real ways within the community.

COMMUNAL CARE   These ethical demands for communal care are central to what it looks like for Israel to be in a covenant relationship with God. In his seminal work on ethics in the Hebrew bible, Jeremiah Unterman notes, "the Lord wants right, not rite . . . 'God requires devotion, not devotions. Sacrifice and prayer cannot serve as substitutes for justice' . . . The revolutionary message of the prophets is that ritual is both secondary to ethics and dependent upon moral behavior for validity."[4] It is not sufficient—to use LDS parlance—to go to church, read the scriptures, and pray daily unless those devotions are accompanied by devotion in the form of protecting the weak. It is not sufficient—to use LDS parlance—to attend the temple and partake of the sacrament, unless those rites are accompanied by doing right for those who are vulnerable. Indeed, Isaiah, Amos, Hosea, and Micah (and Jesus, a true student of the prophets!) all remind us that doing good in our community by embodying *mishpat*, *tsedeq*, and *hesed*—those weightier matters of the law—is not an accoutrement to ritual worship, but rather the foundation upon which ritual worship is built. In sum: these four prophets suggest that if Israel wanted to get square with God, Israel did not need to abandon its worship practices, it needed, instead, to focus on doing the things in their communities that made those worship practices meaningful.

---

4. Jeremiah Unterman, *Justice for All, How the Jewish Bible Revolutionized Ethics*, pp.99, 107. Emphasis removed.

A Quick Diversion on Isaiah

Let me also pause briefly to make a few observations about the Book of Isaiah.

What we know about Isaiah, the man, is scattered in a few places.[5] According to the text, he was an 8th-century BCE prophet, the son of Amoz, and was married to a "prophetess." He had two children (Shear-Jashub, meaning "a remnant shall return" and Maher-Shalal-Hash-Baz, meaning, "spoil speeds, prey hastens") and served the Kings of Judah, from Uzziah through Hezekiah (somewhere between 40–60 years). His prophecies are contemporaneous with Micah (portions of Isaiah's and Micah's prophetic writings are identical), Amos, and Hosea. Though parts of the Book of Isaiah are attributable to Isaiah the man, the weight of Biblical scholarship suggests that other portions of the Book of Isaiah were not written by the man Isaiah but rather by later authors who saw themselves as aligned with his approach.

Chapters 1–39 are pretty clearly within the historical horizon of the 8th century BCE. It is these chapters that most scholars believe were written by Isaiah the man (with the exception of chapters 24–27, the 'Apocalypse of Isaiah' as they are sometimes called; they were potentially written at a much later date). However, beginning in chapter 40, the content, tone, vocabulary, and focus shift slightly, and even the name "Isaiah" stops being used after Chapter 39. Generally, chapters 40–55 seem to be within the historical horizon of the exile in Babylon and aware of the rising Persian threat to Babylon (mid-6th century BCE). This section is sometimes called Second Isaiah or Deutero-Isaiah. Generally, chapters 56–66 seem to be within the historical horizon of the Persian period and the early postexilic period (late-6th century BCE). This section

---

5. See, for instance, Isaiah chapters 1, 6–9 and 36–39.

is sometimes called Third Isaiah or Trito-Isaiah.[6] Though dating is always a little uncertain, it is possible that the writings now in Deutero- and Trito-Isaiah were contemporaneous with some of the writings of Jeremiah, Ezekiel, Malachi, Ezra, or Nehemiah.

So, whether it was a single author or a group of authors, Deutero- and Trito-Isaiah likely represent work that was written centuries after Isaiah's death and that picked up the themes found in Isaiah's original prophetic writings. In a sense, these later writings might be meaningfully seen as an extension of the "prophetic school" of Isaiah.[7] Relevant to this discussion, a key theme (among others) that is carried forward from Isaiah's 8th-century BCE writings and into the worldview of Deutero- and Trito-Isaiah is the notion that worship consistent with the Sinaitic Covenant is properly understood through the socio-ethical demands of communal care. That is to say Deutero- and Trito-Isaiah continue to assert that rite and ritual must be accompanied by *mishpat, tsedeq,* and *hesed.*

---

6. For a very good summary of the historical backdrop of the different parts of Isaiah see Yale Divinity School's Old Testament course material on First Isaiah. https://yalebiblestudy.org/courses/first-isaiah/lessons/historical-context-study-guide/

7. The existence of prophetic schools is attested in the Hebrew Bible. For instance, in one scene, David (not yet king), fleeing from Saul, takes refuge with Samuel. Saul's messengers find a "company of the prophets prophesying, and Samuel standing as appointed over them" (1 Samuel 19:18–24). Later, when the prophetic mantle passes from Elijah to Elisha, the "sons of prophets" from Bethel and Jericho inquire as to when, exactly, Elijah would leave and "fifty men of the sons of the prophets" observed Elijah's departure and see Elisha claim the mantle (2 Kings 2). Later the "sons of the prophets" joined Elisha at Gilgal in the midst of famine (2 kings 4:38–44). These examples, and others like them, suggest that some prophets were not completely isolated, but rather that some had followings. Indeed, at times there may have been a "prophetic guild" of sorts. For powerful prophetic voices, like Isaiah's, it is reasonable to believe that his closest followers continued to work in his name and follow his general approach even after his death.

It is with all this background that we come to the simple and yet profound set of verses in Isaiah 58.

Fasting?

In ways that are reminiscent of Isaiah 1, Isaiah 58 starts with God telling the prophet to speak on God's behalf and to let the people know that God acknowledges the challenges that they are facing (for clarity, I am using the NRSV translation and removing the numbering to better highlight the verses' poetic structure):

> Shout out; do not hold back!
>   Lift up your voice like a trumpet!
> Announce to my people their rebellion,
>   to the house of Jacob their sins.
> Yet day after day they seek me
>   and delight to know my ways,
> as if they were a nation that practiced
>   righteousness
>   and did not forsake the ordinance of
>   their God;
> they ask of me righteous judgments;
>   they want God on their side.
> "Why do we fast, but you do not see?
>   Why humble ourselves, but you do not
>   notice?" (Isaiah 58:1–3a)

According to these verses, God recognizes that Israel seeks God daily. And God also acknowledges Israel's complaint: Israel wants God to be on its side, and to act on its behalf. And God is even aware of the source of Israel's frustration: Israel says that it fasts and humbles itself, but God "[does] not see . . . [and does] not notice." (As an aside, I am confident all of us have felt that way sometimes. "God," we might say, "I am humbling myself and doing the things you ask of me, and yet you do not see me when I cry for help. When will you be on my side and act on my behalf?") So, why isn't God acting on

Israel's behalf if it is doing things, like fasting, that it has been commanded to do? Fortunately, God explains that to Israel. God continues:

> Look, you serve your own interest on
>   your fast day
>   and oppress all your workers.
> You fast only to quarrel and to fight
>   and to strike with a wicked fist.
> Such fasting as you do today
>   will not make your voice heard on high.
> Is such the fast that I choose,
>   a day to humble oneself?
> Is it to bow down the head like a bulrush
>   and to lie in sackcloth and ashes?
> Will you call this a fast,
>   a day acceptable to the LORD? (Isaiah 58:3b–5)

God's criticism is that, in the end, Israel's demonstration of piety and humility through fasting isn't sufficient because the fast is not accompanied by communal care. In fact, God says, the fast is accompanied by actions driven out of self-interest, divisive words and deeds, and results in oppression of those who are lower on the totem pole—all things that God despises. God responds in a way that is refreshingly pointed, effectively asking them: "do you really think that what pleases me is your hunger and the wearing of sackcloth and ashes—is that what you really think this is all about?"

Thankfully, God does not leave Israel without correction. Just as in the other prophetic writings discussed above, God tells Israel what it should be doing:

> Is not this the fast that I choose:
>   to loose the bonds of injustice,
>   to undo the straps of the yoke,
>   to let the oppressed go free,
>   and to break every yoke?
> Is it not to share your bread with the hungry
>   and bring the homeless poor into your house;

    when you see the naked, to cover them
      and not to hide yourself from your own kin?
    (Isaiah 58:6–7)

The "fast" God wants for Israel has nothing to do with the ritual of fasting! God is not concerned with ritual actions, but rather with ethical actions. Rather than focusing on the ritual of going hungry, God wants Israel to focus on the practice of protecting those suffering injustice, freeing the oppressed and breaking every yoke, feeding the hungry with their bread, housing the homeless in their own homes, and covering the naked with their clothes. In short, Isaiah 58 is teaching Israel that exact adherence to ritual requirements is secondary to exercising justice (*mishpat*), righteousness (*tsedeq*), and mercy (*hesed*).

For an exiled people, this would have been a dramatic and challenging requirement. It is one thing, when in exile, to try to keep religious observances. Such acts could be done in secret and without ever reaching beyond the community. Such acts could serve to create separation between Israel and its non-Israelite neighbors. And then, with that piety as a backdrop, one might feel justified in asking God to exercise vengeance on one's behalf against one's oppressors. It is quite something else for God to demand that this exiled people change their focus from ritualist piety to serving their community, including their Babylonian neighbors, In many ways, this charge mirrors Jermiah's prophetic instruction to the exiles that, among other things, they should "seek the peace and prosperity of the city to which [God has] carried you into exile" (Jeremiah 29:7). Isaiah 58 teaches that it is not enough to rely on ritual, even ritual zealously kept. God requires much more.

In Isaiah 58, God offers guidance aimed at helping Israel become true people of the covenant. God says, effectively, "Are there people around you, Israelite or not, who are suffering injustice? Then loose those bonds. Are there people around you,

Israelite or not, who are suffering under the yoke of oppression? Then undo those straps. Are there individuals around you who are hungry, or homeless, or naked? Then feed them, house them, and clothe them, whether they are Israelite or not." Isaiah 58 teaches us that this kind of communal care, not ritualistic hunger, is the "fast" that God required.

After articulating these admittedly demanding requirements, God explains how living this way will impact Israel:

> Then your light shall break forth like the dawn,
>   and your healing shall spring up quickly;
> your vindicator shall go before you;
>   the glory of the Lord shall be your rear guard.
> Then you shall call, and the LORD will answer;
>   you shall cry for help, and he will say,
>   "Here I am." (Isaiah 58:8–9a)

If Israel is able to do these things, God explains, then God *will* go before them and behind them. God *will* vindicate them. And, I think, most touching, when Israel calls for help, the Lord will answer, "Here I am." The Hebrew word for "Here I am" is *hineni*. This is how Moses, Abraham, Samuel, and Isaiah all responded to God's call; God calls, and they each respond with *hineni*. Thus, this word is more than just a statement that one is present and more than an acknowledgement that one is listening. *Hineni* signals openness and willingness; it signals a readiness and responsiveness. It is, in some ways, a promise to action. And this promise to action—the implied promise of *hineni* which God gives to Israel—is, I believe, operative today. Isaiah 58 teaches that as we make our focus on ritual secondary to the qualities of justice (*mishpat*), righteousness (*tsedeq*), and mercy (*hesed*), God will surround us.

As this set of teaching closes, God reiterates to exiled Israel the promise of a return to their homeland, of a future renewal, and of future restoration; a promise that I believe also applies to us still, individually and collectively, as we live through our own exile experiences. Since any commentary I make on these verses would only diminish their beauty, I will let them stand on their own, as they have for thousands of years.

> If you remove the yoke from among you,
>   the pointing of the finger, the speaking of evil,
> if you offer your food to the hungry
>   and satisfy the needs of the afflicted,
> then your light shall rise in the darkness
>   and your gloom be like the noonday.
> The Lord will guide you continually
>   and satisfy your needs in parched places
>   and make your bones strong,
> and you shall be like a watered garden,
>   like a spring of water
>   whose waters never fail.
> Your ancient ruins shall be rebuilt;
>   you shall raise up the foundations of
>   many generations;
> you shall be called the repairer of the breach,
>   the restorer of streets to live in.
> (Isaiah 58:9b–12)

CHAPTER 17

A New Heart[1]

One of the things that I love most about the Hebrew Bible is the boldness of language employed by the ancient prophets. In his seminal exploration of these prophets, scholar, philosopher, and activist Abraham Heschel explains why this prophetic language is so unflinching. Heschel notes: "the prophet hates the approximate, he shuns the middle road . . . [because] the words the prophet utters are not offered as souvenirs . . . In speaking, the prophet reveals God . . . He discloses *divine pathos* . . . [the prophet is] not an instrument, but a partner, an associate of God" (emphasis original).[2] Hebrew Bible prophets, Heschel suggests, do more than just provide guidance; they actually *reveal God* by providing us a sense of how God feels (what Heschel terms 'divine pathos'). Timid language will not do when it comes to revealing who God is and how God feels; there is no "middle road."

Perhaps because the language can feel so jarring, I think it is easiest to see prophetic avoidance of the "approximate" occurring when it comes to the language of condemnation. Whether it's the *Thou shalt nots* of the Ten Commandments

---

1. Portions of this chapter, now modified, appeared in *Public Square Magazine*, "A New Heart I Will Give You," November 1, 2022. Available at: https://publicsquaremag.org/faith/gospel-fare/a-new-heart-i-will-give-you/
2. Abraham Heschel, *The Prophets*, pp.19, 27, 29.

(often called the "Decalogue") or God's unequivocal dismissal of ritual observance that is not accompanied by justice (*mishpat*), righteousness (*tsedeq*), and mercy (*hesed*)[3]—as just two examples—God's not-middle-road-ness comes through clearly and in evocative ways when God is speaking *against* something. In fact, it is the presence of (and prevalence of, if we are being honest) such language that often leads Christians to give the Hebrew Bible short shrift because it feels somehow different from the God they have come to know through the New Testament (and/or, for members of LDS Church, the Book of Mormon, Pearl of Great Price, and Doctrine and Covenants). I believe that Ezekiel chapter 36 remedies this tendency.

Ezekiel 36 is a remarkable chapter of scripture delivered by a prophet in exile and to a people who had suffered the destruction and loss of many of the things that served as cornerstones of their cultural and religious identity—their land, their kingdom, their temple, etc. Yet, what makes this section of scripture of text memorable is not the language of condemnation but rather God's fierce commitment to Israel's restoration. What's more, the not-middle-of-the-road-ness found in Ezekiel 36 culminates in God's willingness to act on *behalf of Israel* (and it might even be said *in spite of Israel!*). Over and against the predisposition to see the Hebrew Bible as a text focused on rules and filled with disapproval for the people's inability to keep those rules, Ezekiel 36 discloses God's deep feelings for Israel and demonstrates that God does not "approximate" when it comes to Israel's restoration. It is a chapter that (true to Heschel's description) is a prophetic disclosure of divine pathos, one in which speaks God passionately in favor of Israel.

But before going further—and recognizing that this section of scripture may be less familiar to some—I will review key

---

3. See the previous chapter of this book. Also see, for instance, Jeremiah 6:10–21; Isaiah 1:10–15; Amos 5:21–27.

parts of it. My focus here is on verses twenty-one through the end of the chapter. The text is below. For ease of reading, I have removed verse numbering, adjusted the formatting, and slimmed down the language. I am using the NRSV translation, but if you'd prefer, please feel free to break away now and read the entire chapter in whatever translation you prefer:

> Thus says the Lord God: It is not for your sake, O house of Israel, that I am about to act but for the sake of my holy name . . . I will sanctify my great name . . . and the nations shall know that I am the Lord . . . when through you I display my holiness before their eyes.
>
> I will take you from the nations and gather you from all the countries and bring you into your own land.
>
> I will sprinkle clean water upon you, and you shall be clean from all your uncleannesses, and from all your idols I will cleanse you.
>
> A new heart I will give you, and a new spirit I will put within you, and I will remove from your body the heart of stone and give you a heart of flesh.
>
> I will put my spirit within you and make you follow my statutes and be careful to observe my ordinances.
>
> Then you shall live in the land that I gave to your ancestors, and you shall be my people, and I will be your God. I will save you from all your uncleannesses, and I will summon the grain and make it abundant and lay no famine upon you. I will make the fruit of the tree and the produce of the field abundant, so that you may never again suffer the disgrace of famine among the nations . . .
>
> It is not for your sake that I will act . . . let that be known to you . . .

On the day that I cleanse you from all your iniquities, I will cause the towns to be inhabited,
and the waste places shall be rebuilt. The land
that was desolate shall be tilled, instead of being
the desolation that it was in the sight of all who
passed by. And they will say, "This land that was
desolate has become like the garden of Eden, and
the waste and desolate and ruined towns are now
inhabited and fortified."

Then the nations that are left all around you shall
know that I, the Lord, have rebuilt the ruined
places and replanted that which was desolate; I,
the Lord, have spoken, and I will do it . . . I will
also let the house of Israel ask me to do this for
them: to multiply their people like sheep. Like a
consecrated flock . . . so shall the ruined towns be
filled with flocks of people. Then they shall know
that I am the Lord.

Fully aware that there are many things in this text that
deserve highlighting, I will focus on three that speak most directly to me and my faith: (1) the reality that God acts; (2) the
fact that God cleanses; (3) and the recognition that there is no
hard division between the spiritual and the earthly.

First, God Acts

Perhaps the most remarkable and distinguishing feature of
this set of verses is the fact that all of the action is attributed
to God: "I am about to act," God says. And act God does:

I will sanctify my great name . . . I display my holiness . . . I will take you from the nations . . . I will
sprinkle clean water upon you . . . A new heart I
will give you . . . I will put my spirit within you . . .
I will save you from all your uncleannesses . . . I
will summon the grain and make it abundant . . . I
will make the fruit of the tree and the produce of
the field abundant . . . I will cause the towns to be

inhabited . . . I, the LORD, have rebuilt the ruined
places . . . I will do it.

That is quite a list! In fact, there is only one action in this
entire section of scripture that is attributed to Israel—the people of Israel are to "ask [God] to do this for them"—every
other action is one that the LORD takes.

In a faith community that is built on the principle that we
should "act and not be acted upon" (2 Nephi 2:26), that embraces hard work and industriousness, and that takes seriously
the now-apocryphal aphorism to "pray as if everything depends
on God and work as if everything depends on you," we can
sometimes forget that (1) God is as invested (in fact, probably
significantly more invested) in accomplishing this work than
we are, and that (2) God has and will continue to act on behalf
of, and often in spite of, us. Yet this is clearly part of LDS teachings. For instance, Joseph Smith wrote that "the standard of
truth has been erected: no unhallowed hand can stop the work
from progressing . . . the truth of God will go forth boldly, no-
bly, and independent."[4] Smith clearly signals that God's truth
will proceed forth independent of any single individual human
action. This sentiment resonates with LDS understanding of
the image of the "stone was cut out of the mountain without
hands" that eventually "filled the whole earth," found in Daniel 2, wherein God's work proceeds under its own momentum
(see also D&C 65:2).[5] Further, in the Book of Mormon's "Allegory of the Olive Tree" (Jacob 5) much of the work of planting
and caring for the various olive trees is attributed directly to
the "Lord of the vineyard." In that allegory, it is sometimes the

---

4. Joseph Smith, *Joseph Smith Papers, History, 1838–1856*, volume C-1 [2 November 1838–31 July 1842]. Available at: https://www.josephsmithpapers.
org/paper-summary/history-1838-1856-volume-c-1-2-november-1838-31-
july-1842/459
5. See also Gordon B. Hinckley. "The Stone Cut Out of the Mountain."
October 2007 General Conference.

case that servants are invited to participate in tending to the garden, but not all actions include servants, and even those that do include servants are clearly instigated and driven by the garden's master. Finally, in the Book of Mormon, God says exceptionally clearly, twice in the space of two verses, "I am able to do mine own work" (2 Nephi 27:20–21).

To be clear, I do not believe the message we should take away is that there is no role for us. Rather, Ezekiel seems to be trying to teach Israel that when it comes to accomplishing God's ends, much of what God intends for us is, frankly, outside of our ability to control. And thus, Ezekiel (a prophet in exile) seems to be saying to Israel (a people in exile): do not lose hope; God will act, and restoration will come; and do not fear because there is no middle-of-the-road-ness when it comes to that promise. God is true to God's word.

That message of hope may be needed today more than ever.

Second, God Cleanses

One of the central critiques that Ezekiel levees against Israel, and the reason he says Israel was eventually exiled, is that "when the house of Israel dwelt in their own land, they defiled it by their own way and by their doings: their way was before me as the uncleanness of a removed woman" (Ezekiel 36:17). For Ezekiel, likely a well-connected, Jerusalem-based priest who worked in the temple and oversaw temple rituals, this language is connected to the notion of moral and ritual impurity (explored in great detail in Leviticus 11–16). Very briefly, the idea is that because Israel engaged in activities that made them both morally impure (e.g., by violating ethical standards) and ritually impure (e.g., by contact with certain things, or through certain bodily functions), the land where Israel dwelled became so tainted that God could no longer remain, and thus Israel was expelled from the land. (As an aside, this seems connected to Israel's understanding of the effect of sin on the temple and the very thing that Yom Kippur sought to remedy, discussed further below.[6]) But, according to Ezekiel, this expulsion from the land is not forever. God will cleanse Israel and the land, and in so doing, set the stage for their return home.

God does this cleansing in two parts. First, God will address Israel's ritual impurity. In most instances (and this is a simplification, but sufficient for this discussion), the process for remedying ritual impurity comes down to "washing and waiting." Whether the impurity comes from contact with a corpse or having a skin disease (for instance), washing that which has become contaminated and waiting a set period of time is how a person moves from being ritually impure to ritually pure. And that is what God will do for Israel. According to Ezekiel, God will "sprinkle clean water upon" the people who have waited in exile. The result is that Israel "shall be clean" from all of its "uncleannesses." In short, God will act to wash Israel and thus to make Israel, again, ritually pure.

Second, God will address Israel's moral impurity. Moral impurity is usually remedied through temple sacrifice (again, a simplification, but sufficient for this discussion), which requires ritual purity. This is why God takes steps to "wash" Israel first. Now that Israel is ritually pure, it is ready for the ordinance that will address its moral impurities. However, since Israel no longer has a temple, it cannot take the steps needed to achieve moral purity. What is Israel to do? Do not despair, Ezekiel seems to say, because God will accomplish this as well! According to Ezekiel, God will help Israel to achieve moral purity through direct intervention. Rather than requiring a sacrifice, God will simply act to change Israel's nature. God will "cleanse" Israel from "all your idols" and give Israel a "new heart" and a "new spirit;" God "will remove from your

---

6. Marc Zvi Brettler. "Day of Atonement (Yom Kippur)." *Bible Odyssey*. https://www.bibleodyssey.org/articles/day-of-atonement--yom-kippur/

body the heart of stone and give you a heart of flesh" and "put [God's] spirit within you." And the result of these many actions on God's part will be that the people will follow God the right way. Remarkably, in this set of verses, there is no action that seems to be directly required on the part of Israel for this to occur. Ezekiel portrays this action as a continuation of God's covenant fidelity to the people of Israel.

This way of talking about "cleansing" runs against the way we sometimes teach about repentance.[7] My experience is that the occasionally imprecise language we use leads to the idea that God cannot cleanse us unless we pass through specific (often neatly alliterated) steps. That is to say, sometimes (contrary to what Ezekiel seems to present) we may unintentionally teach that God's freedom to cleanse us is constrained by, or contingent upon, our specific actions. However, in fact, LDS teachings are fully consistent with Ezekiel's language above. For example, our doctrine accepts that we are all cleansed from the effects of death via Jesus's atonement and not because of any particular step we take (1 Corinthians 15:20–22; 2 Nephi 9:6–13). And when we realize that the Biblical words most often translated as "repent," shub in Hebrew and metanoia in Greek, mean to "turn back" and "change one's mind," respectively, then it be-

---

7. This is not the only place where this idea is present in the Hebrew Bible. For instance, there are similar sentiments in Hosea and in Isaiah 48. And this is echoed in the Book of Mormon (as noted in the Mosiah reference in the body of the chapter), and in the New Testament via the story of Saul/Paul (as just a few examples). In all these instances, it was not the thing they did that made them clean, rather God interacted in the lives of God's people, and because of this interaction the people were motivated to change. Further, it is worth observing that there is no JST qualification to this language. Failing to take this idea seriously by buffet-line-ing the chapter does a disservice to Ezekiel and the Hebrew Bible. As with other writings of Ezekiel, I think he is intentionally bold to drive the point home—an example of his not-middle-of-the-road-ness. Without such language perhaps Israel would be under the mistaken belief that its restoration was something they "earned" rather than a gift that God gave.

comes clear that though we may take steps toward becoming better than we once were, the actual overcoming of past short-comings is not a result of anything we have earned or the inevitable outcome of specific action on our part, but instead a gift that God provides because God is a God of love.

Further to this point, in referencing 2 Nephi 25:23, Elder Dieter Uchtdorf notes potential confusion surrounding Nephi's phrase "for we know that it is by grace that we are saved, after all we can do." He then explains, "I wonder if sometimes we misinterpret the phrase 'after all we can do.' We must understand that 'after' does not equal 'because. . . . We are not saved 'because' of all that we can do. . . . Today and forevermore, God's grace is available."[8] King Benjamin drives this point home most clearly, perhaps, when he notes that even if we serve God in every possible way (including through repentance), we are still unprofitable servants and remain eternally in debt to God's sustaining and saving actions (Mosiah 2:21–24). In short, LDS teachings reinforce, just as Ezekiel explains, that God's freely given actions are the overriding source of our movement from moral impurity to moral purity.

Third, God Connects the Spiritual and the Earthly

Consistent with Ezekiel's view that the actions of Israel tainted the land itself, the cleansing of Israel includes a cleansing of the land. For Ezekiel, as noted above, this is more than just metaphorical. Since the days of the Tabernacle, Israel believed that the sins of the community actually left a "residue of uncleanliness" on the sanctuary (first the Tabernacle, then the Temple). And this "residue" impacted God's ability to dwell in the sanctuary and thus God's ability to be present to them. Extending this notion, Ezekiel asserts that Israel's actions were such that the *land itself*—the land of Israel's inheritance, Jeru-

---

8. Dieter Uchtdorf. "The Gift of Grace." April 2015 General Conference.

salem and its environs—was so tainted by Israel's actions that God could no longer dwell there. So, for Ezekiel, God's act of cleansing Israel from moral and ritual impurity must necessarily include God cleansing the land as well. In so doing, both the people *and* the land would be prepared to receive God's renewed presence.

Ezekiel describes briefly what the cleansing of the land will accomplish. First and foremost, the famines of the past will be washed away, and the land will, again, provide the basic necessities of life; in fact, it will produce abundant grain and fruit. Second, the towns that were previously destroyed will be rebuilt and reinhabited. As noted above, Ezekiel suggests that famine and destruction (both Earthly consequences) were brought upon Israel's people due to Israel's moral and ritual impurity; thus, God's cleansing actions work to restore Israel's wholeness *both* spiritually and physically. But to be clear, this is not just a return to the life-before-destruction-or-famine (Ezekiel notes that pre-exile life was insufficient); rather, God enacts a new creation comparable to the first creation!

Indeed, according to Ezekiel, this reconstitution of the land will be such that the land will become "like the Garden of Eden," a condition in which all human needs are met and during which God dwells with humankind (in Ezekiel 47, a stream miraculously flows from the temple that creates conditions similar to this—hence another connection between creation and the temple and thus between the earthly and the spiritual). In this way, Ezekiel collapses the spiritual and the earthly. Said even more directly, for Ezekiel, there is no hard distinction between the spiritual and the earthly—the two are inseparably connected with regard to both Israel's exile and Israel's restoration.

Again, this view of the relationship between the material and spiritual planes is consonant with modern LDS doctrine. In Doctrine and Covenants 29, there is an extended discussion of God's works, including both the creation and the provision of laws. In both instances, God is clear that while it may be helpful for humankind to make a distinction between the temporal and spiritual, for God, there is no difference. In fact, from God's perspective, as stated in Section 29, "my works have no end, neither beginning"—that is to say, both acts, creation and the giving of laws, are eternal, and they are interconnected. Indeed, in multiple places (and especially in the Doctrine and Covenants), God's work in total is described as "one eternal round" (see D&C 3:1–4 and D&C 35:1, for instance). God's work, described as "my work and my glory" (the immortality and eternal life of mankind, Moses 1:39), requires the creation of an Earth whereon "these [spirits] may dwell" (Abraham 3:24). Further, all ritual religious practices— sacrifice for ancient Israel, and baptism, sacrament, and prayer for Christians— suggests a clear link between physical actions and spiritual outcomes. Even temple work for the dead, a centerpiece of LDS belief and practice, requires physical proxies for covenantal actions and is based on the doctrine that the spirit and the body are the soul of man (D&C 88:15). All of this helps us appreciate the reality that the prophet Ezekiel pointed to anciently: there is no spiritual activity that is not physical, nor physical activity that is not spiritual, and thus cleansing the land and the people are simply different parts of the same action.

For Us Today

In my view, Ezekiel 36 is a wonderful example of what the prophetic language of the Hebrew Bible has to offer us today. As Heschel suggests, in this chapter the historical person known to us as Ezekiel transcends his mortal condition and becomes a true associate of God. In so doing, Ezekiel reveals to us a God who acts to cleanse the people of the covenant and the land where they live. Ezekiel reveals a God driven by divine caring and concern and one who, when it comes to covenant relationship, is even more deeply committed than the children of Israel are. Yet, while this section of scripture is temporally locatable (Babylon in the 6th century BCE), it teaches principles and ideas that extend across time. In Ezekiel 36, we are confronted with the remarkable opportunity to trust that God will do the things for us that we are unable to do for ourselves. The only question is, will we embrace the God that Ezekiel reveals to us?

CHAPTER 18

Bones and Sticks

We know very little about the personal life of the prophet Ezekiel. We know that his name is commonly accepted to mean "God Strengthens." As the Book of Ezekiel opens (Ezekiel 1:3), we learn that he was a priest. It is likely he was a denizen of Jerusalem who served in Solomon's Temple. He was the son of Buzi; Buzi is otherwise unmentioned in the Hebrew Bible. Though there is not complete unanimity on this, I think the weight of biblical scholarship holds that Ezekiel was in Nebuchadnezzar's first deportation of Jerusalem's elite. This deportation occurred in 596 BCE (see 2 Kings: 10–17, 2 Chronicles: 36:9–10; Jeremiah 27:29–20, 29).[1] As a practical matter, this means that Ezekiel was removed from Jerusalem before the temple, and Jerusalem itself, was destroyed.

At the time of Ezekiel's prophetic call, that time when "the word of the LORD came" to him, he was already "in the land of the Chaldeans by the river Chebar" (Ezekiel 1:3). This is to say that he was already in Babylon. This means that Ezekiel's prophesying, for a time, overlapped with the work of Jeremiah (who was operating in Jerusalem). In fact, they may have

---

1. See for instance, Christine Hayes. Open Yale Courses, "Introduction to the Old Testament (Hebrew Bible), RLST 145 - Lecture 19 - Literary Prophecy: Perspectives on the Exile (Jeremiah, Ezekiel and 2nd Isaiah)." There was a second deportation in 587 BCE.

overlapped for as long as a decade, with Ezekiel speaking to those in Babylon and Jeremiah speaking to those in Jerusalem.[2] And, in a remarkable series of early visions captured in Ezekiel Chapters 9–11, Ezekiel sees the God's divine presence rise up and leave the city of Jerusalem, eventually coming to rest "upon the mountain which is on the east side of the city" (Ezekiel 11:23). God, according to Ezekiel, had left Jerusalem. Now, Jerusalem was exposed and ripe for destruction.[3]

It is with this backdrop that we encounter Ezekiel 33:21. The verse is innocuous enough that, unless one is paying attention, its significance might be missed. "And it came to pass in the twelfth year of our captivity, in the tenth month, in the fifth day of the month, that one that had escaped out of Jerusalem came unto me, saying, The city is smitten." *This* is the moment when Ezekiel (and I suppose the others living in Babylon) learns that Jerusalem and the temple had been destroyed. Someone whose name has been lost to history was apparently able to elude the Babylonian army and find his or her way all into the heart of Babylon itself to deliver a message to the exiled community. In my mind's eye I can imagine the breathless, crestfallen messenger speaking these simple words: "The city is smitten."

It is probably hard to overstate the impact the removal of the king, the razing of Jerusalem, and the destruction of the temple would have had on the people of Israel. The Royal Davidic line was subjugated, the city of God was destroyed, and the epicenter of God's presence was violated and dismantled.

---

2. Jeremiah remained in Jerusalem through its destruction, before finally fleeing to Egypt where tradition holds that he died.

3. Not only does the departure of God's presence mean that the city is now unprotected from the Babylonian attack, theologically this suggests that all of the people who remain in Jerusalem—from Ezekiel's point of view—are now without God's presence. It is hard to know for certain, but I think Jeremiah would have disputed this assertion given his continued prophecy during this same time from Jerusalem.

Indeed, "all that seemed theologically guaranteed by [God's] faithfulness, all that gave symbolic certitude, all that was linked to significance, identity, and security was gone."[4] It is hard to find modern-day analogies. The bombing of Pearl Harbor? The attacks of 9/11? Regardless, for Israel, the world as they knew and understood it—socially, politically, and theologically—was forever changed.

This event seemed to be a turning point for Ezekiel. Prior to the fall of Jerusalem, Ezekiel's prophetic oracles grappled with issues that would have been relevant to those in exile, for instance: Where is God (Chapters 1, 9–11)? Why did the invasion happen (Chapters 6–7)? What is the role of individual and communal responsibility for the past and the future (Chapters 4, 18, 33)? The issues of "today." Yet, once Ezekiel hears of Jerusalem's destruction, his prophetic oracles change. Rather than focusing on the right-now, Ezekiel becomes preoccupied, one might even say consumed, with the idea of a future redemption for Israel: the reseating of a Davidic king and reinstitution of the Kingdom of Israel, the reestablishment of the City of Jerusalem, and the rebuilding of the temple. He is so focused on the issues of the future restoration of Israel that all of the writings that come after finding out about Jerusalem's fall, all of the oracles that now comprise Chapters 34 to the end of the Book of Ezekiel, are exclusively focused on these topics.

It is from Ezekiel 37, and from within his preoccupation with the restoration of Israel, that we get Ezekiel's visions of the valley of the dry bones and of the two sticks joined together. As will become evident, each is a rumination on this restoration. I will look at each of these visions one at a time. Because I think it is useful to refamiliarize ourselves with Ezekiel's language, I will first reproduce the relevant parts of the vision (I use the NRSV translation with the verse numbering

---

4. Bruce C. Birch et al, *A Theological Introduction to the Old Testament*, *2nd Ed*, p. 334.

removed), then I will discuss common LDS interpretation, and finally I will look at other ways of understanding the text.

Dry Bones

> The hand of the Lord came upon me, and he brought me out by the spirit of the Lord and set me down in the middle of a valley; it was full of bones. He led me all around them; there were very many lying in the valley, and they were very dry. He said to me, "Mortal, can these bones live?" I answered, "O Lord God, you know." Then he said to me, "Prophesy to these bones and say to them: O dry bones, hear the word of the Lord. Thus says the Lord God to these bones: I will cause breath to enter you, and you shall live. I will lay sinews on you and will cause flesh to come upon you and cover you with skin and put breath in you, and you shall live, and you shall know that I am the Lord."
>
> So I prophesied as I had been commanded, and as I prophesied, suddenly there was a noise, a rattling, and the bones came together, bone to its bone. I looked, and there were sinews on them, and flesh had come upon them, and skin had covered them, but there was no breath in them. Then he said to me, "Prophesy to the breath, prophesy, mortal, and say to the breath: Thus says the Lord God: Come from the four winds, O breath, and breathe upon these slain, that they may live." I prophesied as he commanded me, and the breath came into them, and they lived and stood on their feet, a vast multitude. (Ezekiel 37:1–10)

In a way that is pretty consistent with much of Christianity, LDS interpreters regularly understand this vision to be an expressed reference to the doctrine of the individual resurrection of each person heralded in by Jesus's death and resurrection, i.e. the reuniting of each person's spirit and body into a new, perfect form that is immortal. Indeed, the *Old Testament*

Seminary Teacher Manual says flatly, "Explain that Ezekiel saw in vision the resurrection of many people. Resurrection is the reuniting of the spirit with the body in a perfect, immortal state. A resurrected body is no longer subject to death, so the body and the spirit will never again be separated. . . . Jesus Christ has the power to resurrect us and when we are resurrected, our bodies will be made whole again."[5] That is one way to read these scriptures—and there are many non-LDS Christians who join the LDS community in reading this set of scriptures this way—but this is almost certainly not what Ezekiel intended.

To be clear, there are Hebrew Bible precedents for individuals being raised from the dead. For in instance: God works through Elijah to resuscitate a boy who had died (1 Kings 17:17–24); Elisha raises the son of the Widow of Zarephath (1 Kgs 17:8–24); Elisha also raises the son of a Shunammite woman who showed him hospitality (2 Kings 4:32–37); and a man who had died is revived after his body touches the bones of an also dead Elisha (2 Kings 13:21). But we must remember that none of these instances were resurrection in the sense expressed by modern Christians, but rather bringing individuals from death back and into mortality, i.e. these individuals were not resurrected with a perfect body and into a new, immortal life; instead they were returned to their previous earthly lives in mortal bodies that will die again. Indeed, resurrection as understood by the LDS community does not make its first scriptural appearance until Daniel 12:1–3, a text composed at least a hundred but potentially many hundreds of years after Ezekiel's death.[6] My point is that while the idea of God raising people from the dead was certainly present at and before the time of Ezekiel, the doctrine of resurrection—as LDS and oth-

---

5. "Lesson 142: Ezekiel 37." *Old Testament Seminary Teacher Manual.* The Church of Jesus Christ of Latter-day Saints. Emphasis removed.
6. See also 2 Maccabees 12:44–45, all 2nd Century BCE texts

er Christian believers understand it—simply was not part of Ezekiel's theological horizon. In fact, this notion of resurrection may not have made its way into Jewish thought until as late as the 2nd century BCE (hundreds of years after Ezekiel)[7] when the Judean homeland was at the front lines of a battle between Alexander the Great's successors.

So, if this oracle is not about the doctrine of resurrection, what does it mean? Well, we are quite lucky to have an authoritative explanation of what the oracle means. In a way that is not always the case, God actually provides Ezekiel a clear and unequivocal interpretation of the vision. And God's explanation to Ezekiel has nothing to do with the Christian view of resurrection. In Ezekiel 37:11–14, God explains to Ezekiel:

> Mortal, these bones are the whole house of Israel. They say, "Our bones are dried up, and our hope is lost; we are cut off completely." Therefore prophesy and say to them: Thus says the Lord God: I am going to open your graves and bring you up from your graves, O my people, and I will bring you back to the land of Israel. And you shall know that I am the Lord when I open your graves and bring you up from your graves, O my people. I will put my spirit within you, and you shall live, and I will place you on your own soil; then you shall know that I, the Lord, have spoken and will act, says the Lord.

Summarizing God's explanation to Ezekiel, one commentator notes, "[This] does not involve individual resurrection of the dead. Rather, it concerns the life of the nation: Israel's scattered people, like the scattered bones (37:1–10), will be reunited and will return to the land of Israel (37:11–28)."[8] Ac-

---

7. Michael Coogan, *The Old Testament, A Historical and Literary Introduction to the Hebrew Scriptures*, 3rd ed. pg. 490.

8. Sara Wells. "Ezekiel." Bible Odyssey. https://www.bibleodyssey.org/articles/ezekiel/

cording to Ezekiel's vision, the land that was taken away by foreign invaders, leaving Israel so broken that it was as if Israel's scattered bones lay sun-bleached upon the land, will be miraculously returned to Israel. And it will be God who "places" the Israelites back on their "own soil." That, according to God, is the core message of Ezekiel's vision. In sum, this is a vision of return from Babylonian exile.

It is interesting to note in the preceding verses the way that God will accomplish this miracle. God says: "Thus says the Lord God to these bones: I will cause *breath* to enter you, and you shall live. I will lay sinews on you and will cause flesh to come upon you and cover you with skin and put *breath* in you, and you shall live. . . . Thus says the Lord God: Come from the four winds, O *breath,* and breathe upon these slain, that they may live . . . and the *breath* came into them, and they lived and stood on their feet, a vast multitude . . . O my people. I will put my *spirit* within you, and you shall live" (italics added, Ezekiel 37:5–6, 9, 10, 14). Each of the italicized words above, translated as breath or spirit, is a variation of the Hebrew word *ruach.*

This word, *ruach,* is translated in English variously as wind, breath, and spirit (among other things) in different places in the Hebrew Bible. Notably, it is the word used in Genesis 1:2 to describe God's creative power—God's *ruach* "moved upon the face of the waters" in the very first step of the Earth's creation. The use of *ruach* in Ezekiel's vision ties the power behind the rejuvenation of Israel to the power behind the creation of the Earth itself. Thus, the miracle that Ezekiel envisions is, in some ways, akin to creation itself when God raised humankind from the ground and placed humankind in Eden. Except, in this instance, it is Israel itself that is being raised and returning to the land they were promised; a heritage created (again!) by the very power of God. In both cases, God is working with material that appears formless and chaotic, but which God brings into order and majesty. And if God's *ruach* is sufficient to organize the Earth in this mortal plain, then there is no reason to doubt that God's *ruach* can revive Israel and bring it back from exile to reoccupy its land of promise.

Two Sticks

> The word of the Lord came to me: Mortal, take a stick and write on it, "For Judah and the Israelites associated with it"; then take another stick and write on it, "For Joseph (the stick of Ephraim) and all the house of Israel associated with it"; and join them together into one stick, so that they may become one in your hand. And when your people say to you, "Will you not show us what you mean by these?" say to them, "Thus says the Lord God: I am about to take the stick of Joseph (which is in the hand of Ephraim) and the tribes of Israel associated with it, and I will put the stick of Judah upon it and make them one stick, in order that they may be one in my hand." When the sticks on which you write are in your hand before their eyes. (Ezekiel 37:15–21)

The LDS community understands this vision to be an expressed reference to the coming forth of the Book of Mormon as a companion to the Bible. This interpretive approach is centered on emphasizing the "writing" on "sticks"—one for Judah (the Bible) and one for Ephraim (the Book of Mormon)—and requires reading the oracle with stark literalism. Some Restoration scriptures seem to lend support for this reading. In the Book of Mormon, Lehi (apparently quoting a prophecy from God to Joseph, the youngest son of Jacob, who was sold into slavery in Egypt), says, "Wherefore, the fruit of thy [Joseph's] loins shall write; and the fruit of the loins of Judah shall write; and that which shall be written by the fruit of thy [Jospeh's] loins, and also that which shall be written by the fruit of the loins of Judah, shall grow together" (2 Nephi 3:12). This, coupled with 2 Nephi 29's discussion of the Nephite record as a companion to the Bible and an August 1830 revelation to Joseph Smith identifying Moroni—the final contributor to the Book of Mormon and the one whom Joseph Smith said revealed the location of the golden plates upon which it was written—as holding the "the keys of the record of the stick of Ephraim" (D&C 27:5) has led church leaders to assert, with remarkable univocality and undaunting certainty, that Ezekiel's vision is rightly and properly (and perhaps only) understood as a reference to the Bible and the Book of Mormon.

Indeed, having been raised in the LDS Church and hearing this interpretation repeatedly in my youth, Ezekiel's reference to two sticks seemed to me to be so self-evidently a reference to the Bible and the Book of Mormon that, for a long time, I could not understand how anyone could interpret this vision differently. Interestingly, the LDS community is not the only denomination laying claim to this vision. The Jehovah's Witnesses also see themselves in this set of scriptures and believe that Ezekiel's vision of the two sticks was at least partially fulfilled when, in 1919, "God's people [the Jehovah's Witnesses] were gradually reorganized and reunited" under a series of doctrinal and organizational developments.[9] Again, these are interpretive options, but not what Ezekiel intended.

If we allow our interpretive center to shift away from "writing" on "sticks" and read these verses within the context of the rest of Chapter 37, and with an understanding of Ezekiel's focus on the restoration of Israel, this vision takes on additional meanings. Briefly, it is worth noting that after the united Kingdom of Israel split (following the death of King Solomon), the first king of the Northern tribes was Jeroboam,

---

9. "Questions from Readers: What is the meaning of the joining together of the two sticks described in Ezekiel chapter 37?" *The Watchtower—Study Edition*. July 2016. https://www.jw.org/en/library/magazines/watchtower-study-july-2016/ezekiel-37-stick-judah-ephraim/

an Ephraimite (1 Kings 11:26). The Southern Kingdom, with the remaining two tribes, was led by Rehoboam, a Judahite (and the son of Solomon, 1 Kings 11:43). Hence, in the Hebrew Bible it is not uncommon to see "Ephriam" or "Joseph" used as a shorthand reference for the entire Northern ingdom, and to see "Judah" used as a shorthand reference for the entire Southern Kingdom.[10] So, at the time of Ezekiel's vision, both the northern and southern kingdoms had fallen: Ephraim fell to the Assyrians in 740 BCE (2 Kings 17:6) and Judah fell to the Babylonians in 596 BCE (as noted above). The Kingdom of Israel—the one united, covenant people, comprised of all twelve tribes, led by a Davidic king, that existed free from foreign oppression—was, for Ezekiel, simultaneously a thing of the past and hope for the future.

Ezekiel's vision of sticks builds on the first vision. In Ezekiel's first vision, dry bones are revivified and refleshed by God's *ruach*, signifying a return of the people to the land. But God is not done working. In this second vision, we see God's continued efforts on behalf of Israel. Ezekiel sees two sticks, each named after one part of the divided kingdom; a kingdom that had been separated for more than 150 years. Symbolically, God takes these two peoples and (1) brings them all back together and then (2) reunites them as a single people. So, not only have these separate peoples—Ephraim (and its ten tribes) and Judah (and its two tribes)—all been returned to the land of their inheritance from their various forms of exile and scattering, but they have also been made into "one stick, in order that they may be one in my hand." Like the first vision, God provides an authoritative interpretation to Ezekiel of the symbolism of the sticks. In Ezekiel 37:21–28, God says:

---

10. In a way that can be confusing sometimes, the Northern Kingdom is also called "Israel," at times (not to be confused with the united Kingdom of Israel). One can usually tell the difference by context and the historical period with which the text is concerned.

> I will take the people of Israel from the nations among which they have gone and will gather them from every quarter and bring them to their own land. I will make them one nation in the land, on the mountains of Israel, and one king shall be king over them all. Never again shall they be two nations, and never again shall they be divided into two kingdoms. . . . My servant David shall be king over them, and they shall all have one shepherd. They shall follow my ordinances and be careful to observe my statutes. They shall live in the land that I gave to my servant Jacob, in which your ancestors lived; they and their children and their children's children shall live there forever, and my servant David shall be their prince forever. I will make a covenant of peace with them; it shall be an everlasting covenant with them, and I will bless them and multiply them and will set my sanctuary among them forevermore. My dwelling place shall be over them, and I will be their God, and they shall be my people. Then the nations shall know that I the Lord sanctify Israel, when my sanctuary is among them forevermore.

According to God, this restoration of Israel will be more than just a return to the land (as if that were not enough). It will also entail a return of the people "from every quarter" of their exile and making them "one nation in the land" with "one king," i.e. they will return to a united kingdom. God goes on to say that the newly recreated Kingdom of Israel will never be divided again and will have a Davidic king. The result of this will be "a covenant of peace" where war is a thing of the past. But perhaps most importantly, "My dwelling place shall be over them, and I will be their God, and they shall be my people . . . and my sanctuary is among them forevermore." That is to say, God's presence will return to the land and will fill the sanctuary (i.e. the temple) forever. Ezekiel's vision of sticks, building on the vision of the dry bones, anticipates a full and complete reconstitution of the Kingdom of Israel, reconstruction of the temple (discussed in great detail in later chapters in Ezekiel), and the establishment of a Holy City with Divine presence. That is to say, Ezekiel's visions, when taken together, anticipate a full honoring of the covenant God made with Israel. And for Ezekiel, this does not happen in some sort of esoteric or spiritualized way; this will be a fact of history. Conquered Israel will return to all its glory, and God will make it happen.

Again, it is worth observing that the locus of action is "I"—this is work that God will do. "I will take the people of Israel from the nations . . . I will make them one nation in the land . . . I will make a covenant of peace with them . . . I will bless them and multiply them and [I] will set my sanctuary among them forevermore . . . I will be their God." Each part of the restoration of the Kingdom of Israel is work that God will perform. And if God is acting, what power on Earth can resist?

The Visions Together

Taken together, and understanding Ezekiel's preoccupation with the restoration of Israel, these visions are a powerful attestation of God's future involvement with, and concern for, Israel. Recall that these visions would have been delivered to a people in exile: people whose homeland was taken and destroyed and who were no doubt grappling with despair and hopelessness. That context, in my view, makes these visions even more remarkable. "Do you think Israel is dead and its land lost?" Ezekiel might have asked. "Yet through God's *ruach*—the power of creation—Israel will have its homeland again, as if raising and refleshing dry bones from the earth!" he boldly asserts. "Do you think the Kingdom of Israel is forever gone?" Ezkiel inquires. "Yet God will bring back Ephraim and Judah and make them one kingdom again, as if joining together two sticks!" he proclaims. "Do you think God's presence is forever absent?" Ezekiel queries. "Yet God will reestablish the Holy City and take up residence in the temple once more!" he testifies. For a people suffering through the bleakness of banishment and with no apparent way out, Ezekiel's visions are a profound prophetic call for courage and resolve in the face of seemingly insurmountable obstacles.

And it is the sense of hope that permeates these two visions that I find most compelling. Certainly, we have all faced times when it felt as though we were in exile, without a homeland, and overcome with despair. Certainly, we have all had times when the obstacles that prevented achieving some semblance of control over our own lives seemed insurmountable. It is in these moments that Ezekiel's visions of dry bones and sticks might be needed. In these visions, we are reminded that God's *ruach* can be present in our lives, transforming deathly chaos into unanticipated life. We are reminded that God's commitment to act on our behalf, to gather us and be present to us, never expires even when (and maybe especially when) it seems like there is no way for it to occur. More than just disconnected proof texts for Christian doctrines and LDS scripture, Ezekiel 37 is a multi-verse song of hope raised from the most unlikely of places. And it is a song we desperately need to keep singing today.

Conclusion

Throughout this book, I have I tried to make the case that when we only see the Hebrew Bible through a predetermined lens (including a narrowly-Christian interpretive lens) it robs us of additional layers of insight by depriving us of being able to see how these same texts provided comfort to ancient Israel, are still providing a fountain of hope for modern Jews, and how they can be a fountain of strength and nourishment for us today . . . even those of us who are Christian! I also tried to show that failing to honor multiple readings may unintentionally close us off from seeing *new ways* these texts might be understood in the future, keeping us from seeing the "great and important things pertaining to the Kingdom of God" that are yet to be revealed.[1] Finally, I hoped to reinforce that, in its most pernicious form, failing to honor non-Christian readings (I have actually heard it sometimes expressed in church services as crudely as, "the Jews don't even understand their own scriptures!") is, at its core, anti-Jewish and wrong.

---

1. "Article of Faith Nine." The Church of Jesus Christ of Latter-day Saints. Portions of this chapter, now modified, appeared in *By Common Consent* on April 25, 2023. Available at: https://bycommonconsent.com/2023/04/25/avoiding-antisemitism-in-our-discussion-of-the-new-testament/

This approach takes seriously the advice of Brigham Young that we seek out as much truth as can be learned.[2] As we allow space in our own lives for non-Christian and uncorrelated readings of Hebrew Bible texts, we may find new levels of insight that, perhaps surprisingly, deepen our reserves of Christian faith. We may even find that the ancient and modern worlds have more in common than we initially imagined. Returning to the insights of Walter Brueggemann, he notes: "My own judgement is that it is more important to recognize the commonality and parallel structure of Jewish claims and Christian claims at the core of faith than it is to dispute about which presentation of claim is primary . . . Both faiths have in common [their] common trust in a common God to do something new".[3] By recognizing the many different ways that the Hebrew Bible can be read, we increase our own chance for insight and inspiration and create space to be taught new things.

And this, then, brings us back to considering the Hebrew Bible on its own terms as a complete book of scripture that merits deep and careful study. And as I consider what the Hebrew Bible has taught me, I am drawn back to the remarkable convergence between the message that is embedded in Ezekiel's oracles of bones and sticks and the message of the last verse in the last chapter of the Tanakh: both are foundationally built on hope in God's fidelity to the covenant. But this is not a hope of reward in a far-flung future heavenly realm, but rather a hope that God's fidelity will play out in the lives of God's people here and now. And I want that to be the message the reader is left with in this book, because I see it as a key theme in the Hebrew Bible: *God's covenant is sure. God will always, eventually, provide a way.*

---

2. Brigham Young, *Journal of Discourses,* Vol 16, Discourse 22, Available at: https://journalofdiscourses.com/16/22
3. Walter Brueggemann, *Isaiah Vol 2: 40–66,* pp.143–144.

Throughout the Hebrew Bible, God reaches down to people who are all too human and creates a relationship with them and their families. And then God does it again. And then God does it again. Over and over, God reaches down and God provides a way. Sometimes people abandon God; sometimes they find themselves exiled. And yet, even if they leave God and even if they are exiled, God shows that, despite all odds and despite the people's shortcomings, God will again and again and again extend the power of creation to reconstitute God's people in order to bless of the people of the earth and the earth itself.

It is easy to see why Christians are so eager to claim this message; it is a powerful and life-giving one. But—and we must be clear-eyed about this—this message preceded Jesus's coming. This is the message a young Jewish boy raised in Nazareth in the first century may have been taught by his parents and religious leaders. This God of covenant keeping is the God that a young Jewish boy raised in Nazareth in the first century may have come to know. Eventually, when that young Jewish boy grew up, it is the God that he, Jesus, taught others to come to know. And it is the one we can all come to know better if we really, finally take the Hebrew Bible seriously.

Interpretive Tools

Though it would be disingenuous of me to suggest that going to Wesley Theological Seminary played no role in helping me understand the Hebrew Bible better than I had before attending, one of the things I learned at Wesley is that there are numerous tools that are readily available to anyone who wants to understand the scriptures better. These are tools that do not require attendance at a seminary and which are available to the general public at a negligible or, often, no cost. I want to share with you the tools that I use and which have proven helpful to me.

But before I get to those tools, it is worth acknowledging the elephant in the room. Boyd K. Packer's address to the All-Church Coordinating Council on May 18, 1993, put a voice to more general concerns about the dangers of "so-called scholars or intellectuals."[1] In my experience, within the LDS community, there seems to be a persistent mistrust of people who approach scripture from an academic or non-LDS perspective, particularly when that approach results in conclusions that differ from traditional or common LDS scriptural interpretation. It is likely that this, in turn, results in trepidation when

---

1. See Boyd K. Packer. *Address to the All-Church Coordinating Council,* May 18, 1993. In the same message, Packer identified other "threats" to the Church: feminists and homosexuals.

it comes to using scripture study resources which have not been church approved, or which do not expressly support LDS positions, or which do not come from LDS thinkers or leaders. The idea seems to be that information gleaned from "outside sources" is somehow corrupted or incomplete, or misleading. In my life as a member of the LDS Church, I have experienced these sentiments, to a greater or lesser degree, in every ward I've attended.

However—and I say this with all the emphasis I can muster in writing—it is my belief that *if individuals have any real hope of making sense of the Hebrew Bible, all of these prejudices must be discarded.*

The reality is that there is a world of scholarly resources produced by committed scholars who have dedicated their entire lives to helping us better understand the Hebrew Bible. And, for many of these scholars, this work goes beyond "how I collect a paycheck" and is much closer to a holy vocation—something they feel they have been called by God to do. It is a travesty to disregard their lives' work because of a concern that they might tell us something which contradicts our strongly held opinions or disrupts our commonly accepted scriptural interpretations. In the Doctrine and Covenants, God tells Joseph Smith that God works through holy people that "ye know not of" (D&C 49:8), and I believe those "holy people" can include non-LDS Biblical scholars. So, instead of disregarding the gifts of those who are not of our faith, I think we should embrace what they are offering and utilize it to the greatest extent possible. To that end, throughout this book, alongside my LDS version of the KJV, these are the resources on which I lean most heavily:

❖ A High-quality Study Bible: There are a number of publishers that put out solid study Bibles with meaningful and academically-informed commentary, insights, and essays. For my part, I use two different study Bibles. First, I use *The New Oxford Annotated Bible with Apocrypha*, put out by Oxford University Press. In addition to the Hebrew Bible, the New Testament, and the most commonly accepted apocryphal texts, this publication also includes commentary, a number of essays, maps, a concordance, an index, timelines, chronologies, etc. It is a marvelous resource. It uses the New Revised Standard Version (NRSV) translation of the Biblical text. Additionally, I also use, and find indispensable, *The Jewish Study Bible*, also published by Oxford University Press. This uses the Jewish Publication Society's (JPS) translation of the Tanakh, and also includes wonderful commentary, essays, and other support materials. I use these two study Bibles alongside my LDS version of the King James Version, and the resources it offers. And with these three bibles (the LDS KJV, Oxford's NRSV, and Oxford's JPS) I have an entire library of information, different translations, and study guides. It is not uncommon for me to have all three Bibles open at the same time when trying to understand a given set of scriptures. These study Bibles (and other similarly strong publications) can be found at your favorite online book retailer, at bookstores, and are usually available at the public library if you would prefer not to purchase a copy.

✤ An Interlinear Bible + *Strong's Concordance*: An interlinear Bible is one in which the original text (in the case of this book, the Hebrew text) sits right next to the English text.[2] This allows a word-by-word analysis of how a specific verse is translated. Most helpfully, for those of us who are not fluent in Hebrew (I am cer-

---

2. Biblehub.com also has an Interlinear Greek + *Strong's Concordance* combination for the New Testament.

tainly not), it allows us to start to recognize patterns, understand specific words better, and notice nuances we might not have otherwise seen. (I modeled this in my discussion of the various names used for God earlier.) I highly recommend the use of an interlinear Bible. Relatedly, *Strong's Concordance* is a work of scholarship put together by James Strong that indexes specific words used in the Bible, assigning each a number, so that one can easily cross-reference these words and where they are used (Strong used the KJV for this effort).[3] In the context of my own study, *Strong's Concordance* allows me to look at a specific word (say, *hesed*) and see where that same word is used in other parts of the Hebrew Bible and, importantly, how that same word is used (and translated!) in other contexts. One can find many different interlinear Bibles and copies of *Strong's Concordance* in print and digital versions, but I almost exclusively use the tools available on biblehub.com. Biblehub.com is a free website that has a very handy and also free mobile app. Biblehub.com's interlinear Bible allows one to see both an interlinear version of the Hebrew Bible text (which has to be read from right to left) and links to *Strong's Concordance* at the same time (it also has the *Englishman's Concordance*). I use biblehub.com as much as I use any website on the internet. It is one of the most useful re-

---

3. The complete title of the original work was *The Exhaustive Concordance of the Bible: Showing Every Word of the Text of the Common English Version of the Canonical Books, and Every Occurrence of Each Word in Regular Order: Together with A Comparative Concordance of the Authorized and Revised Versions, Including the American Variations; Also Brief Dictionaries of the Hebrew and Greek Words of the Original, with References to the English Words*. The full-text of the original work can be accessed here: https://archive.org/details/exhaustiveconcor1890stro/page/n11/mode/2up

sources out there for those trying to understand what a specific verse is saying. And it is completely free.

+ Quality Commentary/Analysis: As I noted before, many scholars have spent their lives trying to understand the Hebrew Bible. And often that work is compiled and published in relatively inexpensive volumes. For instance, when I was teaching Gospel Doctrine, as the lessons on Isaiah approached, I secured Walter Brueggemann's two-part collection on Isaiah to help me understand that book of scripture better (I quote from these books in the earlier discussion of Isaiah). Brueggemann's books were exceptionally helpful. That said, it can be hard to search for "books on Isaiah" and know what to get if you are not already somewhat familiar with the names of those who are producing quality commentary. So, one quick trick is to read the essays in the study bibles (which are usually authored by a variety of different, well-respected scholars) and if you like a particular scholar or a particular essay, look for books by that same scholar—or if you find a particular topic interesting, use the bibliography of an essay to find other books on the same topic. Usually, with just a little sleuthing, you can find what you want. And if you have a library card, you can often check out these books for no cost. Though I rank this sort of commentary as a nice-but-not-necessary part of one's Hebrew Bible study, it is the best way to dive in on a specific topic about which you are very passionate and want to explore in greater detail.

That is it. These things can revolutionize one's comfort level and understanding of the Hebrew Bible. Obviously, there are more tools out there, but I think these are the most important and are the tools that I use most often. Analytically, for the preparation of this book, I used these kinds of resources heavily (as my footnotes and bibliography will reflect). Much of what I have come to know about the Hebrew Bible is buttressed by information I have learned from these kinds of sources. I use these resources because they help me better understand what I am reading, and understanding what I am reading brings me closer to God.

Selected Bibliography

"An Apostle Describes a Latter-day Work." 2022. *The Church of Jesus Christ of Latter-day Saints Newsroom*, May 26.

Anderson, Lavina Fielding. 1993. "The LDS Intellectual Community and Church Leadership: A Contemporary Chronology." *Dialogue* 26. 1 (Spring).

Austin, Michael. 2022. "Esau's Embrace: Thoughts on Genesis 33." *By Common Consent*, February 27.

Bell, E. Jay. 1994. "The Windows of Heaven Revisited: The 1899 Tithing Reformation." *Journal of Mormon History*. Vol. 20, No. 1.

Berlin, Adele and Marc Zvi Brettler, eds. 2014. *The Jewish Study Bible*, 2nd Ed., Jewish Publication Society. Oxford University Press.

Bible Odyssey. Society of Biblical Literature.

Birch, Bruce C. et al. 2005. *A Theological Introduction to the Old Testament, 2nd Ed.* Abingdon Press.

Bohn, Robert F. 1984. "A Modern Look at Tithable Income," *Sunstone* 43 (January/February).

Bowler, Kate Bowler. 2019. *Everything Happens for a Reason and Other Lies I've Loved.* Random House.

Brown, Brene. 2021. *Atlas of the Heart.* Random House.

Brown, Natalie Brown. 2022. "Why I Tithe." *By Common Consent*, December 15.

Brown, Victor L. 1974. "I Have a Question." *Ensign*. April 4.

Brown, William P. 2017. *A Handbook to Old Testament Exegesis*. Westminster John Knox Press.

Brueggemann, Walter. 2001. *Deuteronomy*. Abingdon Press.

Brueggemann, Walter. 1998. *Isaiah, Vol 1: Chapters 1–39*. Westminster John Knox Press.

Brueggemann, Walter. 1998. *Isaiah, Vol 2: Chapters 40–66*. Westminster John Knox Press.

Brueggemann, Walter. 1984. *The Message of the Psalms*. Augsburg Publishing.

Brueggemann, Walter. 2001. *The Prophetic Imagination, 2 Ed*. Fortress Press.

Clarke, J. Richard. 1982. "The Value of Work," *General Conference* (April).

Brunson, Sam. 2016. "Understanding 'Interest' in Joseph Smith's Original Tithing Revelation." *Juvenile Instructor*. Feb. 2. https://juvenileinstructor.org/understanding-interest-in-joseph-smiths-original-tithing-revelation/

"Chastity." Topics and Questions. The Church of Jesus Christ of Latter-day Saints.

Come, Follow Me. 2022. The Church of Jesus Christ of Latter-day Saints.

Coogan, Michael D, Ed. 2010. *The New Oxford Annotated Bible, 4th Edition*. Oxford Univ Press.

Coogan, Michael, Ed. 2014. *The Old Testament, A Historical and Literary Introduction to the Hebrew Scriptures, 3rd Ed*. Oxford University Press.

"Elder Bednar Tells the National Press Club About the Church of Jesus Christ." 2022. *The Church of Jesus Christ of Latter-day Saints Newsroom*. May 26.

Eusebius, *Ecclesiastical History*, 4.26. 12, 14.

Finding Strength in the Lord: Emotional Resilience. 2021. The Church of Jesus Christ of Latter-day Saints.

Faust, James E. 1998. "The Windows of Heaven." *General Conference* (October).

Fretheim, Terence E. 1994. "Is Genesis 3 a Fall Story?" *Word and World,* Vol. 14.

General Handbook. 2025. The Church of Jesus Christ of Latter-day Saints.

Givens, Nathaniel. 2022. "The Importance of Prophetic Fallibility." *Public Square Magazine.* May 4.

Givens, Terry. 2015 *Wrestling the Angel.* Oxford University Press.

Givens, Terryl and Fiona. 2012. *The God Who Weeps, How Mormons Make Sense of Life.* Ensign Peak.

"Glossary of Polygamy." 2006. *Deseret News.* June 12.

Green, Arthur. 2012. *Seek My Face: A Jewish Mystical Theology, 2nd Ed.* Jewish Lights Publishing.

Hager, Eli Hager. 2021. "How has Utah Saved $75 Million on Welfare? By Providing Next to None and Taking Credit for LDS Welfare Instead." *Salt Lake Tribune,* December 2.

Harper, Stephen C. 2016. "The Tithing of My People." *Revelations in Context.* The Church of Jesus Christ of Latter-day Saints.

Hayes Christine. "Introduction to the Old Testament (Hebrew Bible), RLST 145." Open Yale Courses.

Heschel, Abraham. 2001. *The Prophets.* Harpur Perennial Classics.

Hinckley, Gordon B. 2007. "The Stone Cut Out of the Mountain." *General Conference* (October).

Holland, Jeffrey R. 1996. "The Peaceable Things of the Kingdom." *General Conference* (October).

Hutchinson, Anthony. 1988. "A Mormon Midrash? : LDS Creation Narratives Reconsidered." *Dialogue.* Vol 21, No 4.

Interlinear Bible: Greek, Hebrew, Strongs. Biblehub.com.

"Isaiah and the Book of Mormon," FAIR Latter-day Saints.

"Jehovah." Bible Dictionary. The Church of Jesus Christ of Latter-day Saints.

Jewish Encyclopedia, 1901–1906. Funk & Wagnalls.

Jewish Virtual Library. American-Israeli Cooperative Enterprise.

Johnson, Elizabeth A. 2024. *Come, Have Breakfast, Meditations on God and the Earth.* Orbis Books.

Johnson, Elizabeth A. 2015. "Jesus and the Cosmos: Soundings in Deep Christology." In Niels Henrik Gergersen, Ed. *Incarnation, On the Scope and Depth of Christology.* Fortress Press.

Keller, Roger R. 2002. "Jesus is Jehovah (YHWH): A Study in the Gospels." In Paul H. Peterson, Gary L. Hatch, and Laura D. Card, Eds. *Jesus Christ: Son of God, Savior.* Brigham Young University.

Kimball, Spencer W. 1976. "The False Gods We Worship." *Ensign* (June).

Kimball, Spencer W. 1980. "The Law of Tithing." *General Conference* (October).

Levine, Amy-Jill and Marc Zvi Brettler. 2020. *The Bible With and Without Jesus, How Jews and Christians Read the Same Stories Differently.* Harper One.

Levine, Amy-Jill. 2006. *The Misunderstood Jew, The Church and the Scandal of the Jewish Jesus.* Harper One.

Lovett, Ian Lovett and Rachael Levy. 2020. "The Mormon Church Amassed $100 Billion. It Was the Best-Kept Secret in the Investment World." *Wall Street Journal.* February 8.

McClendon, Debra Theobald McClendon. 2019. "Discerning Your Feelings: Anxiety or the Spirit?" *Ensign.* (April).

Michaels, David and Jonathan Weil. 2023. "Church of Jesus Christ of Latter-day Saints, Its Investment Adviser Settle SEC Probe." *Wall Street Journal.* February 21.

Milgroom, Jacob. 2004. *Leviticus.* Fortress Press.

Moltmann, Jürgen. 2004. *The Coming of God: Christian Eschatology.* Fortress Press.

Nelson, Russell M. 2003. "Divine Love," *Ensign* (February).

Nelson, Russell M. 2007. "Scriptural Witnesses." *General Conference* (October).

Nelson, Russell M. 2022. "The Everlasting Covenant." *Liahona* (October).

Oaks, Dallin H. 2022. "Introductory Message." *General Conference* (April).

Oaks, Dallin H. 2018. "The Need for a Church." *General Conference* (October).

Oaks, Dallin H. 1994. "Tithing." *General Conference* (April).

Old Testament Seminary Teacher Manual. 2015. The Church of Jesus Christ of Latter-day Saints. https://www.churchofjesuschrist.org/bc/content/shared/content/english/pdf/language-materials/13478_000_OT-Teacher.pdf

Pace, Glen L. 1986. "Principles and Programs." *General Conference* (April).

Packer, Boyd K. 1993. Address to the All-Church Coordinating Council, May 18.

Panikkar, Raimon. 1993. *The Cosmotheandric Experience, Emerging Religious Consciousness* (English Translation). Orbis Books.

Pike, Dana M. and Eliason, Eric A. 2021. "Is the Song of Solomon Scripture?" *BYU Studies Quarterly*. Vol. 60, Iss. 3.

"Questions from Readers: What is the meaning of the joining together of the two sticks described in Ezekiel chapter 37?" 2016. *The Watchtower—Study Edition* (July).

Quinn, D. Michael. 1996. "LDS Church Finances from the 1830s to the 1990s." *Sunstone*. Vol. 102 (June).

Quinn, D. Michael. 1997. *The Mormon Hierarchy, Extensions of Power*. Signature Books.

Quinn, D. Michael, 2002. *Elder Statesman: A Biography of J. Reuben Clark*. Signature Books.

Rasband, Ronald A. 2000. "One by One." *General Conference* (October).

Reiss, Jana. 2020. "On Mormon Tithing and a $100 Billion Investment Fund." *Religious News Service*. December 14. https://religionnews.com/2022/12/14/on-mormon-tithing-and-a-100-billion-investment-fund/.

Roberts, B. H. 2016. *Defense of the Faith and the Saints*, Vol I & II. The Deseret News (Originally 1907 and 1912).

Smith, Joseph, *Joseph Smith Papers, History, 1838–1856*, volume C-1 [2 November 1838–31 July 1842].

Smith, Joseph, *Times and Seasons* (Nauvoo, Hancock Co., IL), 2 May 1842, vol. 3, no. 13, pp. 767–782. Accessed via the *Joseph Smith Papers*.

Spackman, Ben. 2017. "Adam, Where Art Thou?" In Adam S. Miller, Ed. *Fleeing the Garden, Reading Genesis 2–3*. Neal A. Maxwell Institute.

Stapley, Jonathan A. 2018. *The Power of Godliness, Mormon Liturgy and the Cosmos*. Oxford University Press.

Strong, James. 1890. *The Exhaustive Concordance of the Bible: Showing Every Word of the Text of the Common English Version of the Canonical Books, and Every Occurrence of Each Word in Regular Order: Together with A Comparative Concordance of the Authorized and Revised Versions, Including the American Variations; Also Brief Dictionaries of the Hebrew and Greek Words of the Original, with References to the English Words*. Eaton & Mains.

Talmage, James E. 1915. *Jesus the Christ*. Deseret Book.

"Tithing." *Gospel Topics*. The Church of Jesus Christ of Latter-day Saints.

"Tithing." 2004. In *True to the Faith*. The Church of Jesus Christ of Latter-day Saints.

"The Living Christ: The Testimony of the Apostles, The Church of Jesus Christ of Latter-day Saints." The Church of Jesus Christ of Latter-day Saints.

Thompson, Curt. 2010. *Anatomy of the Soul*. Tyndale Momentum.

Uchtdorf, Dieter F. 2015. "The Gift of Grace." *General Conference* (April).

Unterman, Jeremiah. 2017. *Justice for All, How the Jewish Bible Revolutionary Ethics*. Jewish Publication Society.

"Why is Isaiah the Most Quoted Prophet in the Bible?" Chrstianity.com.

MICHAEL HUSTON currently resides in central Maryland. He received degrees from Utah State University (Logan, UT), American University (Washington, DC), and Wesley Theological Seminary (Washington, DC). Though he spent much of his youth west of the Mississippi, he has lived on the east coast for more than twenty years. He and his wife of 25 years have four children